4/96

When Blue Meant Yellow

JEANNE HEIFETZ

When Blue Meant Yellow

How Colors Got Their Names

HENRY HOLT AND COMPANY
New York

This book is lovingly dedicated
to the memory of
Elizabeth Rodgers Dobell,
1936–1992.

Henry Holt and Company, Inc.
Publishers since 1866
115 West 18th Street
New York, New York 10011

Published in Canada by Fitzhenry & Whiteside Ltd.,
195 Allstate Parkway, Markham, Ontario L3R 4T8.

Library of Congress Cataloging-in-Publication Data
Heifetz, Jeanne.
When blue meant yellow: how colors
got their names by Jeanne Heifetz.
p.   cm.
Includes bibliographical references.
1. Colors—Dictionaries, Juvenile.   2. Colors—Nomenclature.   3. Colors—
Folklore—Dictionaries, Juvenile.   4. English language—Etymology—Dictionaries,
Juvenile.   [1. Color—Dictionaries. 2. English language—Etymology.]   I. Title.
QC494.2.H45   1994   535.6'03—dc20   94-6336

ISBN 0-8050-3178-2
First Edition—1994
Printed in the United States of America on acid-free paper.∞

1   3   5   7   9   10   8   6   4   2

When Blue Meant Yellow

ntroduction

Scientists estimate that the human eye can distinguish 7,295,000 shades of color. If we wanted to give each one of them its own name, the whole of the English language, with its approximately 1,000,000 words, would not be enough. The English language does have thousands of names for colors, and some people would say that we have far more names for colors than we need. In the 1960s, two anthropologists in California found that about a dozen basic names describe the majority of the colors we can see: red, yellow, blue, green, orange, purple, pink, brown, black, white, and gray. These eleven names can cover almost all the 7,295,000 visible shades, particularly if you add adjectives like "pale," "deep," "bright," "dull," "light," "dark," "clear," "muddy," and use combinations like "yellow-orange" or "bluish green." (You could probably even do without "pink" if you were willing to call it "pale red" or "whitish red.")

Yet to use only those eleven basic names would be

like eating the same dozen meals for the rest of your life. Yes, we can all understand "Take a left at the red house" without needing to know precisely what shade of red the house is. Even if the road is lined with red houses, "the bright red house with green shutters" or "the dark red house with gray trim" would probably do. But part of the joy of being human is not only noticing that *this* red is not the same as *that* one—but also finding resemblances: one house is the color of burgundy wine, while another is the color of geraniums. You could use "dark red" or "bright red," but why would you want to?

We don't name colors just because we have to, but also because we enjoy doing it. Sixteenth-century France saw such color names as "Rat," "Widow's joy," "Envenomed monkey," and "Chimney sweep." The same period in England saw "Goose-turd green," "Devil in the hedge," "Ladie blushe," "Pease-porridge tawny," and "Pimpillo." "Pimpillo"—pin pillow—meant a pincushion, and by association became the name for the prickly pear; so when the fruit was used as a dye, the color it produced was called "Pimpillo." Eighteenth-century France welcomed "Rash tears," "Paris mud," "Burnt opera house," and "Stifled sigh," while England saw "Elliott's red-hot bullets." By the nineteenth century, "Elephant's breath" had become extremely popular, but sadly, by 1930 no one could remember what it had looked like.

Around the world, people seem to take similar pleasure in naming colors. In one language of the Congo, *elundu*, which we would call light brown, literally means "the color of an anthill." In Samoan, *lanu-moana*, which we could call blue, means "the color of the deepest part of the sea." A Zuñi speaker might describe what we call lavender as "the color of boiled beans," and what we call dark gray as "the color of a mean deer."

What is color? In one sense, color is light. All color comes either directly from a light source or from a surface that reflects light back to our eyes. Color cannot exist without light, so to understand color, you need to know a little bit about light. Light is complicated, but one way to look at it is as electromagnetic energy that moves in waves. The distance between a point on one wave and the identical point on the next wave is called the wavelength. Different colors of light have different wavelengths.

Sunlight, which appears white to us, contains light of many different wavelengths and therefore of many colors. Isaac Newton (see page 69) discovered that he could use a prism to separate sunlight into the colors of the spectrum, and could use a second prism to recombine all the colors of the spectrum into white light. When you mix colors of light, for example by projecting circles of colored light onto a wall, you are adding wavelengths together and producing more light, which is why colors of light are called "additive pigments." The three primary colors of light are red, green, and blue. If you project circles of red and green light onto a wall and move them so that they overlap, the overlapping portion will be yellow. If you project circles of red, green, and blue light, where the three overlap, the light will be white.

Many of the color names you will encounter in the following pages are the names of artists' pigments or dyes, materials artists use to put color on paper or canvas or pottery or to dye yarn or cloth. Pigments and dyes are called "subtractive," because they absorb, or subtract, certain wavelengths or colors from white light, and reflect back the remaining wavelengths. An artist's pigment that looks red has absorbed all the other wavelengths of light and reflects red back to our eyes. The primary colors of subtractive pigments are red, yellow, and blue; if you add all three together, you get black. (In practice, because artists' colors vary, you often get a very dark brown.)

Our eyes have two different kinds of cells that are sensitive to light: rods and cones. The rods enable us to see when the available light is very dim. The cones enable us to see color, but they don't function in dim light, which is why color appears to vanish at dusk or in a dark room.

People around the world all see the same spectrum of colors, but each culture divides the spectrum differently. Some languages, for example, don't have words for colors English speakers would consider basic. Neither ancient Hebrew nor modern Vietnamese has a word for blue. Tagalog has no word for orange. Urdu has no words for orange, pink, or gray. Cantonese has no word for brown, and both the Thai and the Lapps call brown "black-red." Some languages use a single word for colors we consider distinct, like yellow and orange, or blue and green. The ancient Greeks, for example, used the same word for the color of green plants and the color of honey. A single Icelandic word means both black and blue from the color of coal to the color of the sky. The Melanesians of Buin use *tanai* to mean the shades we would call sulphur yellow, bronze, light green, and moss green—because these colors are all present in the leaves and root of the *tana* plant. These combinations aren't too hard to understand, since we see these colors as neighbors in the spectrum. But imagine being the researcher in Brazil who heard a Bacairi woman using the same name, *tu ku éng*, to describe the colors we would call emerald, vermilion, and ultramarine. How could they be related? Well, it turned out that *tu ku éng* was the Bacairi name for a bird with green and blue feathers and a brilliant red spot beside its beak. The bird, a familiar sight to the Bacairi, brought together colors that we think of and name separately. (Our name for the bird, "toucan," comes from the Tupi people, neighbors of the Bacairi.) Would we see the world the same way if we named it differently? If, for example, you never learned that orange was a color distinct from red or yellow (as was the case in English until the sixteenth century), would you *see* orange, or would you only see it as a shade of red or a shade of yellow? It's hard to know, because once you've learned to name orange, it's hard not to see it.

While we try to imagine having no word for blue or brown, speakers of other languages may marvel at the way English uses a single word for colors that their cultures would consider separate. For example, Russian has no single word for what we call blue. Instead, it has one word for light blue, *goluboy* (literally, "dove blue"), and a separate word for dark blue, *siniy*. Italians call light blue *azzurro* and dark blue *blu*. Hungarian has two different ways of saying red, and Hungarian speakers may wonder how we could use one word for both. Some languages also distinguish between *kinds* of color in a way that English doesn't. For example, Samoan has two words for green: Samoans use *lanumeamata*, which literally means "the color of something raw," only for inanimate objects; they use *lanulau'ava*, which means "the color of the leaf of the kava plant," for anything living. Zuñi has two words for yellow: one for the color of something dyed, like clothing or paint; the other for something aged or ripened, like leaves or skin. A Zuñi speaker may well find it strange that we use one word, yellow, for both, and even that we see the two as the same color.

The way a culture names colors tells us something about its history and how it sees the world. For example, ancient Japan had only five words for color, including *kuro* (black) and *shiro* (white); the other three were *akane* (orange), *hanada* (turquoise), and *kariyasu* (yellow). Orange, turquoise, and yellow don't seem like primary colors to us, but these were the colors the ancient Japanese were able to produce from dyes using local plants; the names of the colors came from the names of the plants used to produce them.

When we are very young, we often name colors after things: we may say "chocolate" for "brown," or "chalk" for "white." As we get older, we tend to forget where our names for colors come from. What do the origins of our color names tell us about our own culture? In the pages that follow, you will find colors named after gemstones, metals, spices, wines, fruits, flowers, plants, woods, birds, animals (as well as colors we use only for animals), fossils, the earth, people, cities, and even a battle.

No list of color names can ever be inclusive. New ones are invented all the time; old ones fall out of use. You will doubtless be able to think of a color or two you feel should have been included. I used myself as a test and chose color names that were familiar to me and that I assumed would be familiar to readers. Then I added names whose stories seemed particularly interesting, even if the names themselves were unfamiliar. I hope that if any missing names strike you as you browse through these pages you will be inspired to do some word detection of your own.

Our names for colors reflect the history of English, as you will see as you browse through the entries, particularly the longer essays. This is a book about etymology, the study of words and their origins. Etymology is like detective work. Every English word has a story hidden in it: what language it came from, what it meant in that language, and how it came to mean what it did in English. You will find episodes in the history of English in many of the longer essays in the book. Occasionally you will find quotations from people who spoke an older form of English; the words will be recognizable, but the spelling will give you a sense of how our language has changed over time.

Like people, languages have relatives and ancestors. English belongs to a very large family of languages called Indo-European. You can find a family tree of Indo-European languages on the following pages. People didn't realize how closely related all these languages were until the eighteenth century, when an Englishman noticed the resemblance between words in Sanskrit, the language of the sacred Hindu scriptures and the ancestor of the modern Indian languages, and words of identical meaning in Latin, Greek, Germanic, and Celtic languages. Within the Indo-European family, our language's most important ancestors are a Germanic language called Anglo-Saxon, or Old English; Latin; Greek; and Old French. These languages gave English much of its vocabulary: about one fifth of our words come from Old English; another three-fifths from Latin, Greek, and French. The rest are words English speakers begged, borrowed, and stole from all the places they traveled and from all the people who

Albanian	Armenian	Balto-Slavic	Celtic
Gheg	Armenian	Belorussian	Breton
Tosk		Bulgarian	Irish Gaelic
		Czech	Manx
		Latvian	Scottish Gaelic
		Lithuanian	Welsh
		Macedonian	
		Polish	
		Russian	
		Serbo-Croatian	
		Sorbian	
		Slovak	
		Slovene	
		Ukrainian	

The Indo-European Language Family

Germanic Hellenic Indo-Iranian Romance*

Germanic	Hellenic	Indo-Iranian	Romance*
Afrikaans	Greek	Assamese	Catalan
Danish		Baluchi	French
Dutch		Bengali	Italian
English		Bihari	Portuguese
Faeroese		Gujarati	Provençal
Flemish		Hindi	Rhaeto-Romance
Frisian		Kafiri	Romanian
High German		Kashmiri	Sardinian
Icelandic		Khowar	Spanish
Low German		Konkani	
Norwegian		Kurdish	*All languages
Swedish		Lahnda	listed are derived
Yiddish		Marathi	from Latin.
		Nepali	
		Oriya	
		Ossetic	
		Panjabi	
		Pashto	
		Persian	
		Rajasthani	
		Romany	
		Sindhi	
		Sinhalese	
		Tajiki	
		Urdu	

11

traveled to England, America, and other English-speaking lands. These words come from almost every language on the globe. In the pages that follow, you will discover color names that come from Akkadian, Algonquin, Arabic, Arawak, Armenian, Assyrian, Catalan, Celtic, Coptic, Danish, Dutch, Egyptian, Ethiopic, Flemish, Fulani, German, Guaraní, Hebrew, Hindi, Hungarian, Italian, Malay, Mandingo, Nahuatl, Norwegian, Old Norse, Old Provençal, Old Slavic, Persian, Portuguese, Sanskrit, Scots, Serbo-Croatian, Spanish, Swedish, Taino, Tamil, Tocharian, Urdu, and Wolof. The date after each entry is the first recorded use of the word as a color name in English. The number at the right margin shows you where you can see the color on the chart that appears at the end of the book. The color chart, however, is not intended to represent the full spectrum but only the colors mentioned in this book. To make the chart, I matched the colors in sourcebooks with color swatches. Then, a designer used a computer to turn the hundreds of swatches into a chart. As a result, the chart is only an approximation of the colors named in the text. Some colors share the same number because the distinctions between them are too slight to register on this scale.

You can use this book simply as a reference, or browse through the longer essays—one for each letter of the alphabet. Mysterious and evocative, full of history and lore, these names dazzle us with the wondrous riches of our language and culture.

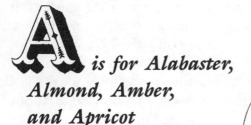

A is for Alabaster, Almond, Amber, and Apricot

Apricot *(1850)*   50

Apricot is one of many colors that take their names from fruits. Legend has it that Alexander the Great was the first Westerner to taste apricots in Asia, where they still grow wild. After his death, his returning armies brought the fruit back to Greece. The Romans, who borrowed much from Greek civilization, imported the fruit to Italy.

At first, believing that apricots originated in Armenia, Romans called them Armenian apples or Armenian plums. (Since apples were the first fruits they knew, the Romans tended to call any new fruit that was similar in shape and size a kind of apple.) But when they discovered that apricots ripen earlier than other fruits, they began to call them *praecox*: *prae* meaning "before," and *cox* meaning "cooked." Although we think of fruit on trees as raw, the Romans thought of it as "cooked" by the sun until it was ripe.

Apricots arrived in England during the reign of

Henry VIII, who wanted every fruit tree known in Europe brought to England to grace the royal gardens at the new Nonsuch Palace. He instructed Richard Harris, fruiterer to the king, to import only the best varieties of fruit, and that included Italian apricots.

When apricots were still a novelty in England, the author of one early herbal, a book of knowledge about plants, thought "apricot" too strange a name for the new fruit. He suggested that the early ripener be called a "hasty peche," but no one listened.

English gardeners continued to search for the best varieties of apricot. One of the most intrepid collectors was John Tradescant, gardener to the Earl of Salisbury and the Duke of Buckingham. Tradescant traveled the world in search of unusual fruits. In 1620, he signed on as a "gentleman volunteer" on a ship bound for Morocco. In those days, the Barbary Coast, the stretch of Mediterranean along the northern edge of Africa, was notorious for "corsairs," pirate ships that plied the waters of the Mediterranean plundering merchant ships of their valuable cargo of spices, silks, amber, pearls, gold, and silver. The armed ship Tradescant sailed on, called a "privateer," was a pirate ship of another sort, sanctioned by the British government to rob the robbers and bring the booty back to England. But Tradescant was not interested in gold or silk or spices. According to one biographer, Tradescant's sole interest in the venture was "finding an opportunity of stealing apricots into Britain." His plan worked. The Algerian variety he carried home became the most popular variety in Britain, and later in the United States, for the next two hundred years. Perhaps in appreciation of his daring service, Tradescant was named Keeper of His Majesty's Garden.

Like Tradescant, the name "apricot" was a world traveler. By the time the fruit arrived in England, its name had already traveled from Latin through late Greek, Arabic, Spanish, Portuguese, and French. In Arabic, *praecox* became *burquq*, receiving the prefix *al*, meaning "the." ("Al" appears in many words we borrow from Arabic, such as "alchemy" and "algebra.") The *l* dropped out of "apricot," but the *a* remains to remind us of the word's long journey. In the seventeenth century, the same Latin roots that gave us "apricot" took a more direct route into English to give us the word we use for a person whose talents ripen early: "precocious."

Absinthe *(1872)* 100
The color of a liqueur made from wormwood, from the plant's Greek name, *apsinthion*.

Alabaster *(1573)* 19
The color of the stone, the highest quality of gypsum. Said to be from *Alabastros*, the Greek name of a town in Egypt where the stone was found, but possibly from Arabic *al baṣrah*, "whitish stones," or "earth out of which they dig stones." The translucent stone was traditionally carved into vessels, and it is also possible that the name comes from Egyptian *a-la-baste*, "a vessel sacred to the goddess Bast."

Alice Blue *(1902)* 145
A color named to honor Theodore Roosevelt's daughter, Alice, whose name comes from the Greek *aletheia*, "truth."

Alizarin Crimson *(1876)* 18
An artist's pigment, first made synthetically in 1868, alizarin is the main coloring material of madder root (see page 88), one of the oldest-known dyes. Its name

comes from the Arabic name for madder, *al 'aṣārah,* "juice," from *'asara,* "to squeeze out, to extract," which describes the process of making the dye from the root. (For crimson, see page 141.)

Almond *(1920)* 48
From the Greek *amugdalē,* borrowed from Hebrew *megedh El,* "divine fruit," or "precious gift from God."

Amaranth *(1690)* 173
The color of the flower, which is as bright dry as it is fresh. From Greek, *amárantos,* "does not fade" or "does not wither," from an Indo-European root that means "to rub, to grind down, to wear away."

Amber *(1500)* 61
From *'anbar,* the Arabic name for the secretion that protects the stomach of the sperm whale from the sharp bones of the cuttlefish (see Sepia, page 124). In French, this waxy substance, valuable for making perfume, became known as *ambre gris,* or "gray amber"; the French called what we know as amber—the fossilized resin used in jewelry—*ambre jaune,* or "yellow amber." They may have thought the two substances were related because resinous amber often washes up from the sea. English adopted the whole name ambergris, but the "yellow" part of *ambre jaune* dropped out, and the resin became known simply as "amber." The most famous amber in the world comes from the countries along the Baltic Sea, where early inhabitants burned amber as fuel. When it burns, amber gives off a scent of pine, and it was later used as incense. An Arabic legend about amber tells of a powerful shah who was extremely fond of pears, but also very impatient. When the shah demanded pears for his table several weeks before they

were ripe, his gardener explained that this was impossible, but the shah threatened to have him beheaded unless he produced ripe pears the next day. The gardener picked some unripe pears and took them to his room, where he locked himself in and spent the night praying and burning amber incense. By morning the pears were ripe, and his life was spared. Scientists have since discovered that burning amber emits ethylene gas, which does indeed speed the ripening of fruit.

Amethyst *(1572)* 170
The color of the gem, from Greek *amethystos*, "not drunk." The Greeks believed that the stone would prevent its owner from getting drunk. (One possible reason for the superstition was that if you drank water out of an amethyst goblet, it would look like wine but not have the same effect.) The root, *methu*, "wine," is related to the English word "mead," a fermented drink made from honey.

Anthracite *(1961)* 190
From the Greek *anthrax*, "charcoal."

Apple Green *(1648)* 92
From Old English *aeppel*, which meant "apple" but was also used for many other fruits; the name may come ultimately from the town of Abella in Italy, famed for its apples.

Aqua *(1941)* 119
From the Latin *aqua*, "water."

Aquamarine *(1598)* 120
The color of the gemstone, from Latin *aqua marina*, "water of the sea." The Roman naturalist Pliny said that

the most valuable aquamarine was "the color of the sea when it is calm."

Ash Gray *(1374)* 98
From Old English, *asce*, meaning the residue left after burning, from an Indo-European root that means "to burn, to glow," and is related to "arid," to be dry.

Auburn *(1430)* 78
Originally from Latin, *alburnus*, "whitish," which is the root of "albino," a person or animal without pigmentation; and "albumen," the white of an egg. English speakers confused this with the French *brun*, or "brown," and so over time the meaning of auburn changed from whitish to brownish.

Aureolin *(1868)* 37
An artist's pigment, from Latin *aureolus*, "little gold."

Aurora Red *(1714)* 55
From the Latin *Aurora*, the goddess of the dawn, ultimately from an Indo-European root that means "to shine," related to our word "east," the direction of the dawn.

Avocado *(1947)* 101
The color of the fruit. From the Aztec language Nahuatl, *ahuacatl*, "testicle," suggested by the fruit's shape. Spaniards altered the name to make it easier to pronounce, perhaps combining it with their word for "delicacy," *bocado*.

Azure *(1374)* 149
From the Persian *lazhward*, "lapis lazuli, blue," perhaps from the mines at Lajward in Turkestan, a source of the stone mentioned by Marco Polo.

*is for Baby Blue,
Banana, Battleship Gray,
Butterscotch, and Buff*

Buff *(1788)*   68

As the fifteenth century drew to a close, traditional armor could no longer offer the protection it had since the Middle Ages. To stop arrows, or bolts from crossbows, or the balls shot from the newly invented guns called the musket and the harquebus, iron armor had to be so thick as to be almost unwearable. Soldiers, particularly those who fought on horseback, began to trade in their cumbersome metal armor for long coats made from the thick hides of oxen, buffalo, and reindeer. This leather took its name from the French word for buffalo, *buffle.*

Buff coats soon became the uniform of the mounted soldiers who were called "dragoons" because the muskets they carried breathed fire, like dragons. Buff leather was as good as armor at protecting soldiers from the thrusts of swords and daggers, and proved a durable material for sword belts and musket straps, strong enough to carry the weight without chafing the soldier's skin. At the coronation of England's King James II in 1685, the

19

gentlemen of the first troop each wore scarlet cloaks lined in blue. Their black hats were edged in silver lace with blue knots of taffeta ribbon (their horses had matching blue ribbons on their heads). To top it all off, each man wore "a good buff coat and a large pair of gauntlet gloves of the same" and was "armed and accoutred with a good broad sword and large buff shoulder belt." Over time, the somewhat unwieldy buff coats became shorter, more fitted vests. But even when cloth uniforms finally replaced buff leather, soldiers favored waistcoats of yellow cloth that imitated the color of buff.

The undyed leather had other uses as well. Watchmakers and silversmiths used small swatches of buff leather to shine metal, so "to buff" came to mean to polish. Since most of the people who wore the buff coats were soldiers, "to be in buff" came to mean to be in the army. But to be "in the buff" meant something very different. Buff coats were made of hide, the animals' bare skins, so naturally, when people were dressed only in their own bare skins, they were "in the buff."

By the middle of the nineteenth century, when most soldiers no longer dressed in buff, firefighters still wore buff coats to keep themselves warm in winter. People who tagged along to see them put out fires would wear buff coats to look like they belonged at the scene. These were known as "fire buffs," and soon a fan or enthusiast of any sport or pastime became known as a "buff."

Baby Blue *(1889)* 121

"Baby" is a very old word, imitating the babbling sounds a baby makes. The custom of dressing male and female children in blue and pink respectively is a relatively modern one. The famous painting *Blue Boy*, by the eighteenth-century painter Thomas Gainsborough, has a companion, if less well-known, painting, *Pink*

Boy. For centuries in most Catholic countries in Europe, all children were dressed in blue from their hats to their stockings and shoes, because the color was associated with the Virgin Mary (see page 139). Outside Catholic countries, white was the generally accepted color for infants. The use of blue and pink began to emerge at the turn of the century, but not as we know it today. In 1918, *The Infant's Department* commented, "There has been a great diversity of opinion on the subject, but the generally accepted rule is pink for the boy and blue for the girl. The reason is that pink being a more decided and stronger color is more suitable for the boy; while blue, which is more delicate and dainty, is prettier for the girl." In 1921, the Women's Institute of Domestic Science in Pennsylvania soundly endorsed pink for boys and blue for girls. A 1930s set of paper dolls, one boy and one girl, came with blue buntings and pink bathrobes for both children; the only sign of the emerging trend was a blue rattle for the boy and a pink one for the girl. By the end of World War II, that trend had completely taken hold.

Bamboo *(1787)*   68
From the Malayan name for the plant, *bambu.* In sixteenth-century Japan, bamboo stems filled with gold dust were official currency. The plant's hollow stems naturally lend themselves to use as musical instruments, from flutes to chimes to xylophones. Perhaps the most unusual use of bamboo occurred when Thomas Edison used pieces of bamboo fiber as the filaments in his early incandescent light bulbs.

Banana *(1923)*   4
The color of the fruit, which came into English through Spanish and Portuguese. Although some sources trace

the name to Arabic *banana*, "finger, toe," it probably has roots in the African languages Wolof, Mandingo, and Fulani, in which *banana* or *baranda* means "plaintain" (a cooking banana). Bananas grow and spread remarkably fast. A Ugandan legend says that the soil of that country was barren until a man named Kintu arrived from the north bearing a single banana root. He planted the banana, and almost immediately, the roots branched out, sending up hundreds of banana plants. The Ugandans, grateful for the sudden bounty, made Kintu their leader.

Battleship Gray *(1916)*   186

An abbreviation of "line-of-battle ship," the most heavily armed warship, "battle" comes from Old French *bataille*, "fight"; "ship" from Old English *scip*, which is possibly related to Lithuanian *skiēbti*, "to rip apart," and Latvian *šķibīt*, "cut, lop," all of which come from an Indo-European root that means "to cut," as you would when hollowing out a log to make a ship. French and German navies first painted their battleships gray in 1895, and other countries soon followed suit. During World War I, gray became the standard color for battleships; this was a form of camouflage, or protective coloring, which became particularly important after the invention of the submarine, which could sneak up on ships in a way that other ships could not. "Camouflage," a word that entered English during World War I, comes from *camoufler*, French thieves' slang for "disguise, deceive," probably from Italian *capo muffare*, "to muffle the head," combined with French *camouflet*, "a puff of smoke blown in the face." Before American battleships were painted gray, their designers tilted the ships' funnels so that their own puffs of smoke would hide them.

Bay *(1374)*   72

From Latin *badius*, a reddish-brown color of horses, through Old French *bai*, and related to Old Irish *buide* and Manx *buigh*, "yellow."

Beet Red *(n.d.)*   **(Beetroot Purple** *1934*) 17

The color of the vegetable's root. Its Latin name, *beta*, probably comes from Celtic, although some etymologists suggest that the beet's shape resembled the Greek letter *beta*, the ancestor of our letter *b*. One variety of beet is actually white, and John Gerard's sixteenth-century herbal recommended that gardeners who wanted the darker color water their white beets with wine. The color of beets does not come from wine but from a pigment called betacyanin, which nineteenth-century women used as rouge. Human beings have a peculiar relationship to betacyanin: a single gene determines whether a person can metabolize the pigment or not. If you inherit from each parent the gene that makes you unable to metabolize betacyanin, then after you eat beets, the pigment will pass right through you: your urine will contain all the beet's color and be bright pink.

Beige *(1887)*   69

From French, *bège*, "gray," used to describe the color of unbleached wool, possibly from Italian *bombagia*, "cotton wool," which in turn goes back to Greek, *bombyx*, "silkworm."

Beryl *(1496)*   118

Both aquamarine (page 17) and emerald (page 46) are types of beryl, a pale green mineral whose name probably comes from Velur, the name of a town in Southern

India. Beryl is probably related to the Tamil *veḷiru*, "to become pale," and also to the Arabic and Persian *ballūr*, "crystal." The earliest spectacles were made from beryl.

Bisque *(1922)* 9
The color of unglazed porcelain; a variant of Biscuit (1884), also a color name, from French *bis cuit* and earlier medieval Latin, *bis coctus*, "twice cooked."

Bittersweet Orange *(1892)* 54
The color of the berries of the bittersweet vine, the roots of which are supposed to taste bitter and then sweet when chewed; from Old English *bītan*, "to bite," and Sanskrit *svādus*, "to be sweet."

Black *(890)* 191
One of the oldest color words in English, from an Indo-European root that means "to shine," or "to gleam." Black is related to words in Germanic languages that mean "ink," which is often black; and words that mean "to burn," since objects often turn black when burned. (See Jet Black, page 72.)

Blond *(1481)* 51
Blond came to English from French, but it ultimately comes from an Indo-European root that means "to flash, to burn, to shine," the same root that gives us blue (see below).

Blood Red *(1297)* 28
See page 98.

Blue *(1300)* 141
Probably from an Indo-European root that means "to

shine, flash, burn," and related to a Latin root that means "blond, yellow." While it may seem peculiar to have one root lead to both blue and yellow, the root probably meant something bright, or brightly shining, and later came to mean specific hues. For further possible etymologies of "blue," see page 29.

Blush *(1590)* 20
From Old English *blyscan*, from a Teutonic root that means "to blaze, to glow," related to Danish *blusse*, "blaze, flame."

Bottle Green *(1789).* 133
After the color of the glass, whose tint comes from the presence of iron oxide. From Latin *buttis*, "vessel, cask," from a root that means "swollen, round."

Brick Red *(1667)* 166
From the French, *brique*, and ultimately from a Teutonic root, *brek-an*, "to break." A brick was originally something broken, a fragment, and came to mean a loaf of bread or clay.

Bronze *(1753)* 65
The color of the metal, an alloy of copper and zinc. From Italian, *bruno*, "brown," and possibly also from the Venetian *bronza*, "glowing coals"; or from the Latin *aes brundusīnum*, "copper from Brindisi," an Italian port town; or from Persian *birinj*, "copper."

Brown *(1000)* 78
An ancient color name, from Old English *burnen*, "burned," and related to "bear," "beaver," and the Greek word for "toad," three brown animals.

Bubble-Gum Pink *(n.d.)* 162

"Bubble" is an imitative word that mimics the sound of bubbling liquid. "Gum," meaning a sticky substance goes all the way back to an Egyptian root, *kmj-t*. Bubble gum as we know it was invented in 1928 by an accountant named Walter Diemer. He colored it pink because he happened to have pink dye lying around, and bubble gum has been pink ever since.

Burgundy *(1881)* 34

The color of wine from the Burgundy region of France; the name "Burgundy" comes from the Germanic tribe called the Burgundii, or "highlanders."

Burnt Orange *(1915)* 44

The color of burnt orange peel; from Old English *beornan*, "to be on fire," and *baernan*, "to set on fire." (For orange, see page 150.)

Burnt Sienna *(1825)* 59

See page 128.

Burnt Umber *(1650)* 72

See page 140.

Butter Yellow *(1909)* 36

Butter comes from the Greek *boutyron*, "ox cheese." The color of butter depends in part on what the cow has been eating. In the early part of the twentieth century, butter yellow referred to a dye made from coal tar that was used to color butter artificially.

Buttercup Yellow *(1883)* 37

The color of the flower, which resembles a cup of butter, and was also believed to give a rich color to butter made from the milk of cows who fed on it. For "butter," see previous page; "cup" comes from Latin *cupa*, "tub, cask, vat."

Butterscotch *(1927)* 43

The color of the candy, which is made from butter (see previous page). Some attribute the name to the candy's Scottish origins, but another possible explanation for "scotch" is the Old French *escocher*, "to cut, to notch," from the lines scored on the surface before breaking the candy into pieces. (The same root gives hopscotch, in which you hop over lines drawn, or "scotched," on the ground.)

**is for Cadet Blue,
Caramel, Cardinal,
Cherry, and
Cobalt Blue**

Cobalt Blue *(1777)*   138

Although English and German are closely related—the original invaders of England, the Angles, Saxons, and Jutes, all spoke Germanic languages—most of the words English has borrowed directly from German are technical terms, and many of them come from mining. Germans have been famous as miners since the fifteenth century. People used to say that a German miner needed only to look at the contours of a piece of land, the colors of the earth, and the plants growing in the soil to be able to tell whether precious ore lay just beneath the surface.

By the end of the sixteenth century, England was full of German miners, who brought their language and superstitions with them. When these workers went into the mines and came out emptyhanded or, worse yet, sick, they said an evil sprite must live in the mine, luring them in with the promise of copper or silver, then stealing the valuable ore and making them ill. They called this sprite a *kobold*, the German word for "goblin." In

English, *kobold* became "cobalt." In mining communities, it became customary for the church service to include a prayer to preserve miners from *kobold*s and other spirits.

It's not surprising that the *kobold* made the miners sick, because cobalt, a metallic element like iron or copper, often occurs in combination with the poisonous element arsenic. Curiously, "blue" also has an association with sickness. While the exact origin of "blue" is uncertain, it may have to come from a root that means "livid," or "bruised"—even though bruises turn many colors as they heal, we still call them "black and blue."

Poison or no, people have been using cobalt to decorate pottery and glass for thousands of years. In the Middle Ages, glassblowers would add cobalt oxide to molten glass, blow the bubble of glass into a long tube, cut off the ends to make a cylinder, and then slit the cylinder down its length. When they unrolled and flattened the cylinder, they had a sheet of intensely blue stained glass, ready to go into a church window. In the fifteenth century, painters discovered that they could take glass colored with cobalt, grind it into a powder, and mix it into a paint: this was the original Powder Blue (1894).

Cadet Blue *(1892)*   139
The color of the uniform worn by officers in training. From French *cadet*, literally, "lesser head," or figuratively, "younger son." A younger son, who would not inherit his family's estate, would often go into the military, first becoming a cadet.

Cadmium Yellow *(ca. 1846)*   40
An artist's pigment, made from the element cadmium, which occurs in zinc, copper, and lead ores. In Latin,

zinc ore was known as *cadmium*, from Greek *Kadmus*, the founder of the city of Thebes, where the ore was found. When the element cadmium was discovered in zinc ore, it seemed natural to borrow the name.

Camel *(1881)* 51

The color of the animal's hair, from Hebrew *gāmāl*, "camel," possibly from Arabic *jamala*, "to bear," because camels are beasts of burden.

Canary Yellow *(1789)* 1

The color of the bird, which is native to the Canary Islands; the Roman natural historian Pliny named the islands *Insulae Canaria*, or "Dog Islands," because of the wild dogs who roamed there.

Capri Blue *(1890)* 115

Capri is an island off the coast of Naples, whose name comes either from Latin *capra*, "goat," or Greek *kapros*, "wild boar." The island is filled with caves, the most famous of which is the Grotta Azzurra, or Blue Grotto, which was discovered in 1828. The Blue Grotto can only be reached by boat because its mouth, which is a little over eight feet in diameter, is almost entirely filled with water. As sunlight passes through the water to the sea bed, about 23 feet below the surface, and is reflected back through the water, a large part of the red wavelengths of light is absorbed, so that the water looks intensely blue, giving the grotto its name.

Caramel *(1909)* 44

The color of burnt sugar. From medieval Latin *calamellus*, "sugarcane" (literally, "cane of honey") combined with Spanish *caramello*, "reed."

Cardinal (1698) 27

Cardinals, whose name comes from the Latin *cardo*, or "hinge," were important clerics on whom the future of the church hinged. Cardinals' skullcaps were traditionally purple, but when Constantinople fell to the Turks in 1453, the secret of purple dyeing (see page 118) was lost to the West. Nine years later, Pope Paul II decreed that dyers should henceforth use kermes (see page 141) to color the cardinals' robes and caps. The brightly colored bird then took its name from these kermes-dyed garments; the color took its name from the bird.

Carmine (1523) 22

See page 141.

Carnation Pink (1535) 11

In Renaissance England, the flower was called "coronation," from Latin *corona*, "crown," either because the flower was used to make crowns for saints' statues, or because the flower itself resembles a crown. After 1600, the name shifted to carnation, from a confusion with Italian *carnagione*, "[light] flesh-colored."

Carnelian (1923) 46

The color of the stone, from Latin *cornus*, "horn," because the stone has the translucence of horn.

Carrot (1684) (Carrot Red) 40

The color of the root, from Greek, *kara*, "head, top," from an Indo-European root that means "head, horn." In Elizabethan and Stuart England, people actually wore carrots on their heads, substituting the greens for feathers in their caps. The original carrots, according to botanists, were probably purple, with later varieties appearing in violet, red, and black. The color we associate with carrots today probably began as a pale yellow variety that resulted from a mutation as late as the sixteenth century. In the seventeenth century, Dutch growers deliberately bred carrots to be a rich orange color. These roots were high in carotene, a natural pigment that provides humans with vitamin A and enhances the color of the cream and butter of carrot-eating cows.

Carthamus Red *(1548)* 27
An artist's pigment, made from the dried petals of the dyer's thistle, also known as safflower, or *Carthamus tinctorius*, ultimately from Arabic *qirṭemá*, "that which is lopped," because dyers pick the buds as soon as they begin to wither. Safflower produced the "red tape" lawyers and government officials used to tie their documents; it also made actors' rouge, and was an ingredient in the Victorian hair oil called macassar, which led to the invention of "antimacassars," pieces of lace that protected upholstery from the staining oil.

Casino Pink *(1928)* 14
From the Latin *casa*, "cottage, hut," the Italian *casino* meant country house. By the eighteenth century, it came to mean a place for social gatherings, and by the mid-nineteenth century, a place where people came to gamble. Since textile manufacturers introduced this color during Prohibition, when it was illegal to sell liquor in the United States, the industry may have hoped to attract customers with a sense of the forbidden.

Cedar Green *(1600)* 100
From Greek *kedros*, "cedar"; possibly from Hebrew *qetoret* "smoke, incense." Cedar would thus be "the wood burned for incense." In the first century B.C.E.,

furniture made of cedar wood, with its striking grain called tigered or pantherine, became the fashion in Rome, worth more than its weight in gold. One Roman writer called this fashion an "extravagant mania." The cedars of Lebanon have been famous since biblical times, and in 1737 the botanist Bernard de Jussieu, brother of Joseph (see page 63), traveled to Lebanon to bring back a cedar seedling. On his return journey, the ship he was in was blown off course, and was soon running out of fresh water. Everyone was put on a ration of one glass of water a day. Jussieu shared his ration with the tiny plant. Not having a flowerpot with him, Jussieu planted the seedling in his hat, and when he finally returned to France, the customs officers thought he was smuggling contraband. They wanted him to dump out the contents of his hat, but Jussieu convinced them to let him keep the seedling planted. He carried it to the Botanic Gardens in Paris, where the cedar grew to be eighty feet tall and lived for one hundred years, until it was cut down to clear a path for a railway line.

Celadon *(1768)* 122
A color of porcelain named after the ribbons worn by Céladon, a shepherd who loves Astrée in *L'Astrée*, a French romance by Honoré d'Urfé (1568–1625). Céladon was named in turn for a character in Ovid's *Metamorphoses;* ultimately from Greek *keladōn*, "to roar like the sea or wind."

Cerulean *(1590)* 140
From Latin, *caeruleus*, derived from *caelum*, "sky, heaven." Although it literally means "sky-color," *caeruleus* could mean either "dark blue" or "dark green." Latin writers used it primarily to describe the sky and the Mediterranean sea, but also leaves and fields.

Chalk White *(1400)*   182

From Latin *calx*, "small stone, pebble, limestone." (See Zinc White, page 156.)

Chamois *(1766)*   68

The color of the leather made from the skin of this antelopelike animal, whose name comes from an ancient Alpine language, ultimately from an Indo-European root that means "hornless."

Champagne *(1915)*   7

The color of the drink, from the Champagne region of France, ultimately from Latin *campania*, "plain, field."

Charcoal *(1606)*   189

The "char" in "charcoal" may come from a Middle English word meaning "to turn," because charcoal is wood "turned" into coal. More likely, the word combines Latin *carbo*, "glowing coal," which became *charbon* in French, with Middle English *col*, "coal, glowing ember," possibly from a Sanskrit root that means "to glow, to blaze, to burn."

Chartreuse *(1884)*   102

The color of the liqueur made by Carthusian monks. Both the liqueur and the order take their name from the French town of Chartrosse, where St. Bruno founded the religious order in the eleventh century. The monks started manufacturing the liqueur from brandy, hyssop, angelica root, and other herbs in 1607.

Cherry *(1447)*   14

The color of the fruit, whose name may come from Cerasus in Pontus, where they were grown, or from Greek *keras*, "horn," because of the smoothness of the tree's bark. Or the name may be of Semitic origin, from Akkadian *karshu*, "stone fruit." The French for cherry, Cerise (1858), is also used as an English color name.

Chestnut *(1555)* 78
The color of the nut, from Greek *kastanea*, derived from the Armenian name for the tree, *kaskeni*. Most chestnuts in America were destroyed in the great blight that began in the Brooklyn Botanic Gardens in 1903, but chestnuts in Europe escaped the disease. Chestnut is one of the color terms often used for horses. Coincidentally, the most famous European tree was the Italian *Castagno di Cento Cavalli*, or "Chestnut of the Hundred Horses," which grew in Sicily on the slopes of Mount Etna, and whose trunk was 190 feet around. The tree's name comes from a story about Jeanne of Aragon, who was traveling to see Mount Etna when a fierce storm forced her and her retinue to seek refuge under the giant tree, which kept all one hundred horses and their riders dry.

Chocolate *(1737)* 81
From the Mexican Nahuatl language, *xococ*, "bitter," and *atl*, "water." The original hot chocolate was not sweet at all, but a frothing mixture of cocoa beans, annatto and anise seeds, crushed red peppers, and cinnamon. When Hernando Cortez arrived in Mexico, the Aztec emperor Montezuma, whose household consumed two thousand jars of chocolate a day, served his guest chocolate in a goblet made from beaten gold.

Cinnamon *(1679)* 75
The color of the spice; the inner bark of a relative of the laurel tree. From Hebrew *qinnāmōn*, probably from Malay *kāyu mānis*, "sweet wood."

Citrine *(1386)*   104

The color of the stone, a variety of quartz. From the fruit citron (see below).

Citron *(1430)*   103

The color of the fruit, a relative of the lemon, ultimately from Latin *citrus*, "citron tree." The name may possibly come from a confusion of the tree with the cedar, because both have aromatic wood. Citrons are one of the four plants carried during the Jewish Feast of Tabernacles. The Talmud tells of a high priest in the second century B.C.E. who deliberately mocked tradition by spilling water meant for the altar on the ground. The congregation responded by showering him with the citrons they had been holding for the service.

Claret *(1547)*   165

The color of the wine, which comes from French *vin clairet*, or "pale wine."

Clay *(1594)*   71

From an Old English word *clǣg*, from a root which means "to stick, to cleave," and is related to "clammy" and "glue."

Clove Brown *(1705)*   72

The color of the spice, a dried flower of an evergreen tree; from French *clou*, "nail," which the spice resembles. The trees are native to the Molucca Islands, once known as the Spice Islands and now part of Indonesia. The inhabitants of the Moluccas used cloves as a mark of dignity; an important person was said to have one, two, three, or four cloves.

Cocoa *(1887)* 73

From an Aztec word, *cacahuatl*, "cacao seed," which became *cacao* in Spanish, and "cocoa" in English, used to make chocolate (see page 35). The Aztecs used bags of cacao seeds as money.

Coffee *(1695)* 82

The color of the beverage; from Arabic *qahwah*, which originally meant "wine," possibly from a root that means "to have no appetite." Since Islam forbids alcohol, coffee became known as the wine of Islam, and was said to have cured Mohammed of narcolepsy (sleeping sickness). The name of the drink may also come from Caffa, or Ethiopia, where the coffee plant grows wild. An Ethiopian legend recounts that a goatherd named Kaldi became curious about the berries that his goats liked to eat, because they seemed so lively afterward. He sampled the berries and discovered that they had a similar effect on him. He brought the berries to his religious teacher, who was delighted that at last he had a way to keep people awake during the lengthy evening prayers. (The French phrase for coffee with milk, Café au lait [1839], has also become a color name in English.)

Copper *(1594)* 46

The color of the metal. From Greek, *Kuprios*, the island of Cyprus, where copper was found in abundance.

Coral *(1513)* 25

The continuous skeleton of undersea polyps, coral takes its name from Greek *korallion*, "red coral," perhaps from Hebrew *gōrāl*, "pebble, small stone used for casting lots," and Arabic *jaral*, "pebble." Often used for jewelry, coral comes in at least 100 different shades of red, including one jewelers call "angel's skin."

Cordovan *(1925)* 79
The color of a type of leather from Córdoba, Spain, where an extensive leatherworking industry was founded by the Moors.

Cornflower Blue *(1891)* 152
The color of the flower, so named because it is found in cornfields. "Corn" comes from an Indo-European root that means "kernel, grain"; "flower" from an Indo-European root that means "to thrive, to bloom." In 1806, when Queen Louise of Prussia fled from Napoleon's army, she took her children to hide in a cornfield where she passed the time, and kept the children quiet, by weaving cornflower wreaths. Sixty-five years later, one of those children defeated France in battle and had himself crowned emperor of Germany at the French palace of Versailles, where he declared the cornflower to be the symbol of his triumphant nation's unity.

Cranberry *(1942)* 33
The color of the fruit, from Low German *kranbere*, "craneberry," from the plant's beaklike stems. "Crane" comes from an Indo-European root that means "to cry hoarsely," also the root of "crow." "Berry" comes from an Indo-European root that means "to shine."

Cream *(1500)* 6
"Cream" has several roots: Greek *khrisma*, "anointing," which came to mean "consecrated oil"; Latin *cremor*, meaning "the juice of boiled grain," from *cremare*, "to burn"; and possibly a third, Celtic root, related to Mid-

dle Irish *scram*, "surface, skin," and Welsh *cramen*, "scab," since cream rises to the surface of milk.

Crimson *(1400)* 17
See page 141.

Currant *(1899)* 32
The color of the fruit, from Anglo-Norman *raisins de Corauntz*, "grapes of Corinth," because currants were initially confused with the tiny dried grapes exported from the Greek city.

Curry *(1946)* 61
The color of the seasoning, from Tamil *kari*, "sauce, relish for rice." Curry is actually a mixture of spices; its color comes from turmeric, whose name may come from the Persian-Arabic *kurkum*, "saffron," or from Latin, *terra merita*, "deserving earth." Turmeric was used to dye silk and wool in Asia, Greece, and Rome.

Cyan *(1879)* 112
From Greek *kyanos*, "dark blue enamel, lapis lazuli." Related to Hittite *kuwanna*, "copper, copper blue, ornamental stone."

Cypress Green *(1905)* 88
From the tree's name in Greek, *kyparrissos*, which is probably related to the Hebrew *gōpher*, the wood from which Noah is said to have made the ark. In the Zoroastrian religion the cypress, whose leaves point toward the sky, was the first tree in Paradise, and the sparks that lit the first fire came from the top of the cypress tree. Zoroastrians planted cypresses in front of their temples as a reminder of the lost Paradise.

D *is for Daffodil Yellow, Damask Red, Delft Blue, and Dapple Gray*

Dapple Gray *(1386)*

Cultures often develop specialized color names to describe the plants or animals that are central to their livelihood. The Ovaherero, a herder people of southwest Africa, developed dozens of color words for the colors of their cattle, but found the idea of having words for blue and green "highly amusing." Perhaps, said one psychologist, if cows came in blue and green, they wouldn't think having names for these colors so silly.

The Mursi, herders in southern Ethiopia, have color names only for the colors of cattle. When a researcher asked one Mursi man to name a large number of colored cards, the man used the names of cattle colors for all of them. For the blue or green cards, for example, he used the closest cattle color: *chagi*, the name of a bluish-gray cow. When the researcher gave him a card and he couldn't come up with a cattle color for it, he said, "There's no such beast!"

While English is not rich in cattle colors, it is rich

in names of colors for horses. Both in England and in America, horses were once much more important than they are today, not only for transportation but also to do heavy labor in the fields. A vestige of those times is the variety of our color names for horses: bay (page 23), chestnut (page 35), dun (page 45), palomino (page 105), and sorrel (page 129). (These are, of course, names for the natural colors of horses. In the sixteenth century, the Turkish practice of dyeing the manes, tails, and legs of white horses red spread to Europe. Well into the twentieth century, Arabs still used henna, a plant dye, to turn the hair of white horses red. For more about henna, see page 65.)

Animals are not always a single color, and we also have many words for the pattern of colors, or markings, of an animal's coat. For cats, we use "tortoiseshell" to describe a mixture of brown, black and yellow fur, from Late Latin *tortuca*, "tortoise," whose root means "twisted," and shell (see page 127). "Brindled," meaning tawny or gray with dark streaks, comes from a root meaning "burned." "Tabby," a striped gray or tawny coat, comes from the characteristic multicolored fabric of Al-Attabiyeh, near Baghdad. "Calico," which describes an animal with red or black markings on a white background, comes from the patterns of fabric made in Calicut, India. Today we use calico to describe cats, but it was originally a term for horses, as are "piebald," "skewbald," and "dapple gray." Piebald, which usually refers to a black-and-white spotted horse, comes from the Welsh *bal*, meaning "streaked with white" and Latin *pica*, "magpie." *Bal* combines with a Scandinavian root, *skeu*, "sky," to form skewbald, a brown or red horse with irregular light markings.

"Dapple gray" has a more puzzling history. Old

Norse, German, Dutch, French, and even Russian all have words that mean *apple*-gray: *apalgrār, apfelgrau, appelgrauw, gris-pommelé, yablokakh*. Since these color names almost always described horses, it seems likely that "apple-gray" meant a horse whose gray coat mimicked the splashes of color on an apple, or a gray horse with round, apple-shaped spots. So how did "apple-gray" become "dapple-gray"? Well, it wouldn't be the first time a word beginning with *a* got a *d* stuck onto it: "daffodil" started out as "asphodel." "Asphodel" became "affodil," and then "the affodil," which, said fast, shrank down to "daffodil." Perhaps "the apple-gray horse" became "dapple-gray horse."

But the origins of words are not always completely clear, and the answer to the puzzle of "dapple-gray" may lie elsewhere. In 787, Norse and Danish Vikings began raiding England. These violent invasions continued until the year 878, when King Alfred defeated the Vikings, and came to a peaceable settlement with them: the northern half of the country came under Scandinavian rule and became known as the Danelaw. By 1014, England had a Danish king, Cnut.

The Angles, Saxons, and Jutes were in fact closely related to the Vikings. Their languages weren't very different. Old Norse, the ancestor of modern Icelandic, Faroese, and Norwegian, was a close cousin of Old English. So in the period of the Danelaw, neighbors speaking the two languages often found that they could communicate, particularly if they compromised on the sounds of words.

In Old Norse, *depi* or *depill* meant a small pool or puddle, and came to mean a dog with a splash or spot of color above its eyes. So at some point, "apple-gray" probably got mixed up with the Old Norse *depill* to form "dapple-gray." A famous horse of Norse legend was a dapple-gray: the giant, magical Dapplegrim, whose hooves carried him straight up walls, his gray coat gleaming like a looking glass.

Daffodil Yellow *(1860s)* 37
The color of the flower, from its Greek name, *asphodel*. The initial *d* probably comes from Dutch: *de affodil*, or "the asphodel." (See previous page.)

Dahlia Purple *(1886)* 172
The color of the flower, which is native to Mexico, where it was sacred to the Aztecs, who associated dahlias with the body of the Feathered Serpent, Quetzalcoatl. The flower is named for Anders Dahl, an eighteenth-century Swedish botanist and pupil of Linnaeus (see pages 94 and 142). When a French botanist named Menonville was in Mexico trying to collect species of the cochineal bug (see page 142), he asked what plant he should use to provide food for the creatures. The answer was "the red-flowered cactus," but he misunderstood and thought he should bring the red-flowered dahlia. The insects perished for lack of food, but the dahlias arrived safely. Napoleon's wife, the empress Josephine, started cultivating the flowers, and even held a dahlia reception for diplomats to admire her handiwork. At the reception a Polish prince bribed the gardener to procure a hundred tubers for him so that he too could grow the spectacular flowers. Josephine was furious at the betrayal and gave up her hobby.

Damask Red *(1588)* 166
The color of cloth from Damascus, the Syrian city famed for its silks; the city's name comes from Hebrew

dam, "blood," because it is, in legend, the place where Cain killed his brother, Abel.

Damson *(1667)* 179

From the color of the fruit, whose name is a contraction of Damascene plum: the plum of Damascus (see previous page).

Dandelion Yellow *(1919)* 36

The color of the flower. From French *dent de lion*, or "lion's tooth," describing the leaves' jagged edges. The flower was traditionally known as a natural clock whose petals opened between five and six in the morning, and closed between eight and nine at night. Some people believed the flower was even more precise, opening at six minutes past five o'clock and closing at nine minutes past eight.

Davy's Gray *(1800s)* 188

An artist's pigment made from powdered slate.

Delft Blue *(1800s)* 151

A color found often in the glaze of pottery and tiles from Delft, in the Netherlands, which has made earthenware since 1310. The town's name means "canal," from the same root as "delve" in English.

Delphinium Blue *(1919)* 142

The color of the flower, from Greek *delphin*, "dolphin," from the shape of the flower's nectaries. The origin legend of the Pawnee people tells the story of the first delphinium. It seems that an old woman was in the heavens spinning dreams so that they would be ready whenever the gods wanted to send a dream to a mortal.

Curious about these mortals, she poked a hole in the sky to see them, but they were still very far away, and she wanted to see them up close. The material she spun into dreams was not strong enough to make a cord to lower her to earth, so she broke off a piece of the sky, which was blue underneath and green above. She spun a cord and dropped it through the hole, but the sun turned the cord brittle and it broke into thousands of pieces. The pieces fell to the earth, turning into the green stalks and blue flowers of the delphinium.

Dove Gray *(1705)* 159
The color of the bird, possibly from a Germanic root that means "to dive" or an Indo-European root that means "to fill with smoke, to darken."

Drab *(1686)* 69
From Late Latin *drappus*, "cloth," possibly related to Welsh *drab*, "a thing torn off."

Duck Green *(1789)* 135
The color of the bird, from Old English *dūce*, from a root that means "to duck, to dive."

Dun *(953)* 67
A Celtic color name used for animals, particularly the mouse, the cow, and the ass. From the same Indo-European root as "dusk," dun is related to Old Irish *donn* and Welsh *dwn*, "dark"; Old Saxon *dosan*, "chestnut brown"; Old English *dosen*, "chestnut horse"; and Old High German *dosan*, "pale yellow."

E is for Ebony, Eggplant, Electric Blue, and Emerald

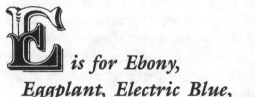

Emerald (1598) 130

"Emerald" came into English from French, but its root is a Semitic word meaning "to flash" or "to glisten," related to the Hebrew, Arabic, Aramaic, and Akkadian words for lightning. This root became *marakta* in Sanskrit, *smáragdos* in Greek, and *émeraude* in French. Like their name, the most famous emeralds in the ancient world came from the Near East: "Cleopatra's mines" in Egypt near the Red Sea were large enough to hold four hundred miners at once. Turtles made of emerald decorated the doors of Cleopatra's palace, and if you were one of her favorites, she would give you her portrait engraved on an emerald.

In the sixteenth century, Spanish conquistadores discovered emeralds in South America, and stole thousands of emeralds from the natives of what are now Peru, Ecuador, and Colombia. These included a people the Spaniards called Esmeraldas, the Spanish name for emeralds, because the gems were plentiful in their jewelry.

The Esmeraldas, who were weavers and potters as well as silversmiths and goldsmiths, are now extinct, but the tale they told of the origin of emeralds survives:

In the days before people used calendars to measure time, huge animals roamed the jungles and fish the size of whales filled the waters. The whole earth was wilderness, except for a few tranquil mountainside groves, created by the Goddess of the Trees. There order reigned.

Then people came to live on the earth. The animals fled from these new enemies, retreating deep into the jungle. They discovered the goddess's peaceful forests, stripped the trees of their bark, and ate the tender green leaves. The Goddess of the Trees begged the powerful god Ches to save at least one of her forests from destruction. She told him that when one day humans put down their bows and arrows, they would start hunting for beauty. Where would they find it if not a single green forest was left? Ches was not happy to see the forests harmed, but he refused to intervene, telling her that all things on earth must change.

Soon great floods covered the earth. The few people who survived began to pray for the first time, thanking the gods for sparing their lives. The Goddess of the Trees heard their prayers and wanted more than ever to show them beauty. She gave them sunrise and sunset and the music of brooks and birds. But she still wished they could see her trees as they had been.

Her sister, the Goddess of the Grotto, came flying toward her across the sky, offering a gift to the people of the earth. She told the Goddess of the Trees to turn the white crystals that lined her grotto's walls into the shimmering green of her own forests. Then people would always be able to come to the grotto and see their beauty.

The goddesses flew together to the mountain cavern.

The Goddess of the Trees was overwhelmed by the beauty of its sparkling crystal walls. Unwilling to transform all that her sister had made, she picked out a few chambers and turned their walls into a brilliant green ice. Sunlight played on the green stones as though on new leaves.

Then the sisters heard thunder. The grotto shook and trembled. The two sisters flew out of the cave into the sky. Looking down, they saw the caverns explode. Crystals flew across the earth. Rain flooded the earth for five days and nights, and the grotto disappeared. The sisters had defied Ches, and this was his revenge.

But many years later, when the people who survived the second flood gathered together in friendly tribes, Ches showed them where the fragments of the grotto lay buried in the earth. These emeralds were their gift from the Goddess of the Trees.

Ebony *(1590)* 84
The color of the wood, from the Egyptian name of the tree, *hebny*.

Ecru *(1869)* 68
A French word for the color of unbleached fabric, from Latin, *crudus*, "raw."

Eggplant *(1915)* 35
The color of the fruit, whose name comes from its shape; "egg" goes back to an Indo-European root that means "bird"; "plant" from a root that means "to spread." Eggplants originated in Asia, and the first varieties to reach Europe were round and white, hence their name. This color is also called Aubergine (1794), the French word for eggplant, ultimately from Persian

bādingān, which one etymologist translates as the vegetable that does not upset the stomach, an unlikely way to describe an eggplant.

Eggshell *(1941)* 7
From "egg" (see previous page); and Old English *sciell*, "peel, rind, husk, eggshell."

Electric Blue *(1884)* 115
The color of an electric spark. The Greek word for amber was *ēlektron*, because rubbing amber on a surface produced static electricity. The Greek philosopher Thales is said to have been the first to discover this property. When watching his daughter spin on a spindle made of amber, he noticed the way the amber attracted stray threads. (The Persian name for amber literally means "abductor of straw.") Later Greek scientists discovered that if they rubbed amber with a woolen cloth in a darkened room, it would give off blue sparks, like tiny bolts of lightning. "Electric" is related to the Greek *elektros*, "gleaming, shining, brilliant," *ēlektōr*, "beaming sun," and perhaps to the Sanskrit *ulkā́*, "meteor."

is for Fawn,
Fir Green, Fire Engine Red,
Forget-me-not Blue,
and Flamingo Pink

Flamingo Pink *(1897)*   10

In the sixteenth century, English sailors began exploring
the globe in search of spices, silks, and dyes. Out on the
ocean they crossed paths with ships from the great sea-
faring powers of the age. They met Spaniards in the
West Indies, Mexico, and South America; and Portuguese in East Africa, India, and China. Bits and pieces
of the Spanish and Portuguese languages made their
way into English. In 1565, an English sailor in Florida
first saw a river bird "having all redde feathers," and
borrowed the name the Spanish and Portuguese sailors
had given it: *flemengo.*

Some people say that "flamingo" comes from the
Latin word *flamma*, or "flame," the color of the birds'
startling plumage. But most people think that the Spanish and Portuguese sailors were making a joke, compar-
ing the birds' color to the florid complexions and bright
clothes of the Flemings, the people of Flanders, now
part of Belgium.

No one knows whether the Flemings got their ruddy cheeks from what they ate and drank, but the flamingo is living proof of the adage that you are what you eat. The brilliant color of the birds' legs and feathers comes from carotene, a natural pigment responsible for the color of dandelions, marigolds, pumpkins, sweet potatoes, and (of course) carrots. The color of egg yolks and butter also comes from carotenes; the depth of the color depends on what the chicken or cow has been eating.

Flamingos get beta-carotene from the tiny mollusks, crustaceans, and blue-green algae in their diet. Like baleen whales, flamingos have bristlelike filters inside their mouths that work like nets to help them extract food from silt and mud.

In ancient Egypt, the flamingo was the hieroglyph for the color red. ("Hieroglyph" comes from the Greek for "sacred writing," and describes the pictures Egyptians used to represent sounds and words.) But the birds' color is not permanent, as the curator of birds of the Bronx Zoo discovered when he led an expedition to the Andes and brought back several rare flamingos, only to have them lose their color the first time they molted. In captivity, if flamingos don't get the proper diet, their feathers and legs will fade to white. The curator experimented with various foods, and discovered that healthy doses of carotene—in this case, carrot oil—could restore their flaming color.

Fawn *(1789)* 69
The color of a young deer, from Latin *fetus*, "offspring, newborn animal." Related to Old Provençal *fedon*, "lamb." The soft, speckled coloration of a fawn acts as camouflage on the light-flecked forest floor.

Fern Green *(1902)*   100

From a Sanskrit root, *parṇa*, meaning "wing, feather, leaf."

Fir Green *(1884)*   128

From Middle English *firre*, probably from a Scandinavian root, ultimately from an Indo-European root that means "oak." In Russia, one grove of fir trees was the site of a rain-making ritual: three men would climb a fir tree (on average, a fir tree is a hundred feet tall); one would imitate thunder by banging on a kettle; another would rub sticks together to make sparks for lightning; and a third would dip twigs into a vessel of water and sprinkle droplets to make rain.

Fire Engine Red *(n.d.)* (Fire Department Red *ca. (1912)*)   28

The earliest hand-pumped fire engines in America were not always red—far from it. Volunteer fire companies received their rigs in gray and then vied with each other to decorate them. In New York, one company's engine was plum with carmine wheels and blue panels; another's was green and yellow with hand-carved dolphins on the sides; a third was royal blue with gold trim. The elaborate paint jobs inspired the expression "All dressed up like a fire engine." At Engine Company #3, when the firemen talked about repainting the company's engine, one man, who loved the way the company's pea-green rig stood out against the snow, shouted, "I don't care what color you paint her, so long as you paint the old gal green!" From that day forward, whenever Company #3 put out a fire, people said they'd "painted it green." The now-familiar red became popular in the 1850s with the rise of the steam-pumped engine, but did not become the most common color until the advent of the motorized fire engine in the early years of the twentieth century. American LaFrance, one of the leading manufacturers of fire equipment, began to offer vehicles in Fire Department Red, although dark maroon also remained a popular color. In 1953 *Science News* reported that one out of ten fire engines was *not* painted red; they even mentioned a "lilac number." In the early 1970s, some departments switched to "lime yellow" because it was supposed to be more visible at night, but many firefighters rejected the garish color; in Boston, firefighters won passage of a city ordinance that all city fire equipment would henceforth be red.

Flake White *(n.d.)* 183
An artist's pigment made from flakes of white lead, in a process in use since the fourth century B.C.E. The method involved casting molten lead in strips, placing it in glazed earthenware pots with vinegar, then burying the pots in horse dung for a month. The rotting dung provided both the heat and the carbon dioxide necessary to the process. "Flake" is probably related to the Old Icelandic *flā*, meaning "to flay, to skin," from an Indo-European root that means "to be flat," which entered English through a Scandinavian word meaning "the sole of the foot."

Flame *(1590)* 56
From Latin *flamma*, "flame," from an Indo-European root that means "to shine, flash, burn."

Flax *(1915)* 68
The color of the plant from which linen is made, either from an Old Teutonic root *flah*, "to braid," or from a root that means "to flay," because the plant must be soaked and stripped to obtain the fiber. In Scandinavia,

flax is sacred to the sky goddess Hulda, who always loved to watch women spinning and weaving wool. One year she came down to the earth at midsummer to watch them work, but found them with empty hands. She asked them why they were not working, and they explained that until the sheep were shorn again, they had nothing to spin and nothing to weave. In an instant Hulda covered the ground with flax and taught them how to turn the plant into linen.

Flint Gray *(1000)*   186
One of the oldest English color names, from the color of the stone used to make blades and create sparks for fires. From an Indo-European root that means "to split, to cleave," and related to the Swedish *flinta*, "stone splinter," and the Greek *plinthos*, "tile."

Fog *(1922)*   185
From Danish *fog*, "shower, mist, spray, drift of snow."

Forest Green *(1810)*   134
From Latin *fors*, "outside, out of doors." Related to *fores*, "door," the root of "foreign."

Forget-me-not Blue *(1877)*   150
The color of the flower, whose name is a translation of the Old French *ne m'oubliez mie;* the flower was supposed to keep loved ones in mind. One version of the origin of the name is that after Adam named all the plants and animals in Eden, he warned them to remember what they were called. One poor flower forgot and called out, "What's my name?" Adam replied, "Forget-me-not."

Forsythia *(1925)* 36
The color of the flower, an early spring blossom; forsythia is native to China and takes its English name from the Scottish botanist William Forsyth, who served as royal gardener to George III and domesticated the flower in England.

Fox *(1796)* 71
The color of the animal's fur. From German *fuchs*, "fox," which comes from an Indo-European root that means "bushy, shaggy," and related to Sanskrit *púčhas*, "tail": the fox is the bushy-tailed animal.

Fuchsia *(1892)* 15
The color of the flower, named for the sixteenth-century German botanist Leonhard Fuchs.

G *is for Gamboge,*
Geranium, Gold,
Government Wall Green,
and Garnet

Garnet *(1783)*   174

Garnet is a gemstone whose name comes from a fruit,
the pomegranate. In Latin, *pomum granatum* means
"many-seeded apple." Garnets looked so much like the
luminous seeds of the pomegranate that *granate*, the
name of the seed, became "garnet." Pomegranate also
gave us the word "grenade," which is both shaped like
a pomegranate and filled with many seedlike grains of
powder; and "grenadier," a soldier who specializes in
throwing grenades.

For centuries, people believed that garnets gave off
both light and heat. An old-fashioned English name for
garnet was "carbuncle," from the Latin *carbo*, meaning
"glowing coal," the root of our word "carbon."
Archelaus, king of Cappadocia, said that if you used a
garnet as a signet ring, it would melt the sealing wax.
According to Jewish legend, Noah hung a garnet in the
ark and the stone glowed brightly even during the darkest hours of the flood. In the fifteenth century, an En-

glish alchemist named John Norton proposed building a golden bridge over the Thames in London. Instead of using lanterns to light the bridge, Norton suggested using garnets on golden pinnacles.

In the Middle Ages, Scandinavians told the story of the miraculous garnets in the giant rose windows of the church at Visby on Gotland, overlooking the Baltic Sea. At night the garnets shone like the sun at noon, guiding sailors safely home. In 1631, the king of Denmark attacked the town and stole the precious garnets. During his escape, the treasure ship carrying both the king and the garnets was wrecked. The king survived, but the garnets sank. Afterward, mariners said that an eerie rose-colored light shone from the garnets at the bottom of the Baltic Sea.

The sea really does contain garnets. If you've ever walked on a beach after a storm and noticed a purplish cast to the sand, you were seeing thousands of tiny garnets washed up on the shore. Perhaps that's the reason the Caribs of the West Indian island of Dominica told the tale of a giant garnet embedded in the forehead of a huge underwater snake. Most of the time, a thin skin like an eyelid veiled the stone, but when the snake left its nest to eat or swim in the deep, it would open the eyelid and use the "wonderful lustre" of the jewel to light its way in the ocean's depths.

The Roman natural historian Pliny would not have been surprised by this story. He himself described a garnet called *draconitis*, which "forms in the brains of dragons." Philostratus, a Greek philosopher who lived at the turn of the third century, added that a garnet taken from the head of a mountain dragon would make the wearer invisible. Naturally, people wanted to know where they could get such a stone. The problem was that the garnet had to be taken from the head of a live dragon, or, as Pliny instructed, removed "immediately after their heads are cut off." In 1502, an Italian physician wrote you could get draconitis in the East, where "bold Fellows" sought out the dens of dragons and strewed the grass around the den with a sleeping potion. When the dragon ate the drugged grass and fell asleep, they cut off its head and procured the stone. Some lucky people didn't have to go to all that trouble. In 1509 a Swiss man was working in his field when he thought he saw a dragon flying overhead. He fainted in terror, but when he came to, he found the dragon stone at his feet. No one mentioned whether the stone enabled him to disappear, but as late as 1723 the magical garnet was reputed to cure virtually all diseases.

Gamboge *(1634)* 62

An artist's pigment made from the resin of a tree found mainly in India, Thailand, and Sri Lanka. From the French for Cambodia, *Cambodge*, which comes from Kambu, the legendary founder of the Khmer people.

Gentian *(1925)* 150

The color of the flower. According to the Roman historian of science Pliny, the flower was named for Gentius, the king of Illyria in the second century B.C.E., who discovered the flower's medicinal properties: the root, perhaps the bitterest known, is said to aid digestion and reduce fevers. Legend has it that when Ladislas was king of Hungary, the country was beset by the plague; the desperate king shot an arrow in the air and begged God to have it point the way to a cure. The arrow landed in a gentian root, which Ladislas is said to have used thereafter with much success to cure the plague. Although gentian does not contain any substance known to cure the plague, it was used throughout the Middle Ages as an antidote to various poisons, and in later centuries as an antiseptic.

Geranium *(1842)*   26
The color of the flower. From Greek *geranos*, "crane," because the flower's seed pods resemble a crane's beak. In Islamic legend, Mohammed wore garments woven from the fibers of the mallow plant (see page 89) and liked the cloth so much he gave the plant brilliant red flowers, turning it into the geranium. Another version of the legend says that Mohammed was washing his shirt in a stream and hung it on a mallow plant to dry. The plant blushed at the honor the Prophet thus bestowed on it, turning bright geranium red.

Ginger *(1552)*   75
The color of the spice, from Sanskrit roots *śṛṅgam*, "horn," and *vera*, "body," because of the hornlike shape of the root. Marco Polo brought ginger from Asia to Europe. British colonists carried the precious root to America, and even used ginger cookies as bribes for votes in early Virginia elections.

Gold *(1400)*   64
From an Indo-European root, *ghel*, "to shine" or "to be yellow." In Greek and Roman legend, gold was mined by many creatures, from tiny ants to enormous griffins, mythical beasts with the head of an eagle and the body of a lion. The Scythian people, famous as goldsmiths, were said to be perpetually at war with the griffins, who jealously guarded gold mines. Pure gold as it comes from the mine, also called 24-carat gold (from

the Greek *keration*, a weight whose name is a diminutive of *keras*, "horn,") is too soft to be useful in jewelry, so goldsmiths make mixtures, or alloys, of gold and other metals. The content of the alloy affects the color of the jewelry. Eighteen-carat gold, for example, is seventy-five percent gold and twenty-five percent other metals, often a combination of copper and silver. More copper than silver produces an alloy called "red gold." When silver predominates, the result is "green gold." Goldsmiths use nickel or palladium, with a little zinc and copper, to create the alloy known as "white gold."

Goldenrod *(1915)*   36
The color of the flower, a combination of "gold" (see previous page) and the Old English *rod*, "twig." During the American Revolution, goldenrod tea replaced the black tea the colonists had dumped overboard during the Boston Tea Party.

Government Wall Green *(1950)*   96
A color standardized by the federal government's General Services Administration for use in official buildings.

Grape *(1916)*   171
Grape Green *(1893)*   100
The colors of the fruit, whose name comes from French *grappe*, "bunch." In French, *grappe de raisins* means a bunch of grapes, but English uses the French word for bunch to mean grape, and uses the word that actually means grape for the name of the dried fruit. Grapes have grown wild in North America for many centuries. When the Viking explorer Leif Ericsson landed on the Atlantic coast around the year 1000, he named the continent Vine Land.

Graphite *(1915)* 189

A form of carbon that is the "lead" in pencils, graphite takes its name from the Greek *graphein*, "to write," which originally meant "to scratch," and is related to the English word "carve."

Grass Green *(700)* 85

See page 145.

Gray *(700)*

Grāeg is an Old English word, related to words in Old Norse, German, and Swedish that mean "dawn," which makes it likely that the word originally referred to the pale colors of the world at sunrise. This idea is not limited to Germanic languages; in the language of the Native American Klamath people of southwestern Oregon, "gray" is *päkpä'kli*, which is related to *pä'kgti*, "the morning dawns."

Green *(700)* 117

See page 145.

Greige *(1906)* 109

From French *grège*, meaning "raw, undyed silk cloth."

Gunmetal *(1870s)* 188

"Gunmetal" generally refers to an alloy of copper and tin or of copper and zinc. "Gun" is a shortened form of the Old Norse woman's name Gunnrhildr, or "war-battle," given to an early stone-throwing weapon; "metal" comes from Greek *metallon*, "mine, mineral, metal," from a root that means "to seek out."

H is for Hansa Yellow, Hazel, Henna, Hyacinth, and Heliotrope

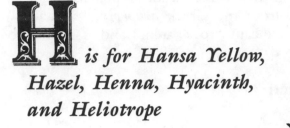

Heliotrope *(1882)* 178

Heliotrope is the color of a flower whose name comes from the Greek words *helios*, meaning "sun," and *tropein*, "to turn": heliotrope is the flower that turns toward the sun. In Greek legend, the heliotrope was once a sea nymph named Clytie. The Greeks envisioned the earth as a flat disk floating like an island in a river ruled by Clytie's father, Oceanus. By day, Helios, the sun god, traveled across the sky from east to west in his golden chariot, drawn by four snow-white horses. At night he returned from west to east, traveling across the ocean in a giant golden cup.

Clytie and Helios fell in love, but Helios soon abandoned her for Leucothea. When Clytie told Leucothea's father what had happened, the enraged king had his daughter buried alive. But even the death of her rival did not console Clytie. For nine days she sat on the cold riverbank and watched Helios travel across the sky. For nine nights she waited while he sailed around the earth in his golden boat. She ate nothing. She drank nothing but her own tears and the morning dew. At the end of nine days she turned into the heliotrope flower, which follows the sun as it makes its way across the sky.

In time, of course, people realized that the world was not flat but spherical, and scientists began to wonder how large the earth really was. In 1735 the French Academy of Science sent a team of scientists to South America to measure a degree of meridian—1/360th of the earth's circumference—at the equator. Joseph de Jussieu, who came from a family of famous botanists, traveled with the delegation. He spent the next fifteen years in the Andes studying plants, including cinchona, whose bark provides quinine, the cure for malaria; and canella, whose bark we know as cinnamon. When he discovered in Peru the flower we know as heliotrope (a different flower from the one the Greeks called by that name), he was "intoxicated with delight."

Just before Jussieu was to return to France, his entire collection of plants and seeds was stolen. Fifteen years' worth of work had disappeared. The shock drove him crazy. Luckily, he had already sent seeds of the heliotrope to his brother in Paris, where the plant became known as the "love-flower," and people thought only the most beautiful and expensive vases worthy of it.

Hansa Yellow *(1934)*   37
The trade name for a painter's pigment invented in Germany; *hanse* is German for a merchants' guild.

Harvest Gold *(1923)*   4
From Old English *haerfest*, "picking time," or "autumn," related to the Latin for "to pluck, gather" and the Greek for "fruit."

Havana Brown *(1875)* 66
The color of cigars, for which Havana, the capital of Cuba, is famous.

Hazel *(1592)* 75
The color of the nut, from the Old English *haesl*, related to Old Lithuanian *kasulas*, a hunting spear made from hazel wood. In Greek myth, however, a hazel rod denotes peace: Hermes's caduceus, a winged wand entwined with serpents that had the power to heal and reconcile people divided by hatred, was made of hazelwood. Today the caduceus is a symbol for medicine.

Heather *(1918)* 161
The color of the flower, whose name comes from the Scottish *hadder;* the *th* came from a confusion with *heth*, a Middle English word meaning "uncultivated land."

Hemp *(1917)* 107
The color of rope made from the twisted fibers of an Asiatic plant; the name comes from the Greek name for the plant, *kannabis*. Canvas, a fabric made from hemp or linen fibers, gets its name from the same root. The plant and its name may originally have come from Asia: Herodotus mentions the Scythians growing hemp. In one of Aesop's fables, the owl tries to warn the other birds about the dangers of this new plant, but they ignore his wise counsel, and soon men are using the plant's fibers to make snares to trap the birds. Although the plant is also the source of marijuana, it was grown in England by royal edict in order to provide rope for the ships of the British navy. One variety of the plant, Manila hemp, takes its name from the capital of the Philippines. Coarse Manila hemp was used to make

ropes, sails, and mats; the finer grades became handker-
chiefs, scarves, and even the sturdy paper whose color
we also call Manila (1892).

Henna *(1613)* 78

From the Arabic name for the dyeplant *hinnā'*. The ancient Egyptians used henna to dye their nails, their
palms, and the soles of their feet. Today henna is primarily used as a hair dye, although in many Muslim cultures the palms of a bride's hands and the soles of her
feet are elaborately decorated with henna designs before
her wedding to bring her luck. Moroccans also use
henna to paint the sign of the hand of Fatima, Mohammed's beloved daughter, on their doorposts, to protect
their homes.

Holly Green *(1898)* 132

From an Indo-European root that means "to prick,"
and is related to the Russian *kolos*, "spike, ear of grain."
In fact, only the leaves of a young holly tree have prickly
edges to protect them from foraging animals. When the
tree has grown taller and the leaves are out of reach of
animals, the edges of the leaves become perfectly
smooth.

Honey *(1611)* 63

From Old English *hunig*. The name of the substance itself may come from its color: "honey" is related to the
Greek *knēkos*, "pale yellow, saffron," Old Prussian
cucan, "brown," and Welsh *canecon*, "gold."

Honeydew *(1925)* 52

The color of the juicy melon, from "honey" (see above)
and a Sanskrit root, *dhávati*, "it runs, it flows."

Honeysuckle *(1921)*   51
The color of the flower, from "honey" (see previous page) and Old English *sūcan*, "to suck," which comes from an Indo-European root that means "to take liquid."

Hooker's Green *(1820s)*   85
A watercolor pigment named for William Hooker, a botanical artist who lived from 1779 to 1832.

Horizon Blue *(1905)*   145
The color of the sky at the horizon, the place where the sky and earth appear to meet. "Horizon" comes from the Greek *horos*, meaning "boundary," and *horizein*, "to limit." Horizon blue was the color of French military uniforms during World War I, presumably because they were hard to see against the sky.

Hunter Green *(1872)*   129
From Old English *huntian*, "to chase wild animals and game," related to *hentan*, "to try to seize or capture." Hunters presumably wore dark green in the woods to conceal themselves from their prey.

Hyacinth *(1920)*   (Hyacinth Blue *1388*) 156
The color of the flower, named for a Greek prince loved both by the god Apollo and the west wind, Zephyrus. According to legend, Apollo and Hyacinth were throwing the discus together when Zephyrus, out of jealousy, blew the discus straight into Hyacinth's skull, killing him. Apollo created the flower from the slain youth's blood. Some Greek writers said that the markings on the petals spelled out *ai, ai,* or "woe, woe," Apollo's lament. According to Ovid, hyacinths still droop in the wind because of the fatal wind-borne blow.

Hydrangea Blue *(1899)*   157
Hydrangea Pink *(1905)*   10

The color of the flower, which ranges from blue to pink depending on the acidity of the soil in which it grows. From the Greek *hýdōr* and *angeîon*, meaning "water" and "vessel," because the seed pods resemble small cups.

is for Ink,
Isabelle Color,
Ivory, Ivy,
and Indigo

Indigo *(1289)* 143

Indigo is one of the oldest dyes in the world. As early as 4,500 B.C.E., Egyptians were using indigo to dye the cloth they used to wrap mummies. In Greek, the dye plant's name was *indikon pharmakon*, or "Indian dye." The dye's name comes from the country, and the country's name from the river Indus, which in turn takes its name from the Sanskrit *syand*, meaning "to flow."

Many cultures have used indigo to dye cloth. The Tuareg people of the African Sahara were often called "the blue people" because of their fondness for veils and robes dyed with indigo, whose color often rubbed off on their skin. In Liberia, West Africa, people tell the tale of Asi, the woman who first learned the secret of indigo dyeing. Asi's heart, the legend explains, was "hungry for color." She envied the *veda* bird, whose color came from rubbing against the sky. In those days, the people say, the sky hung so low that people could touch it. They could even tear off pieces of the sky and eat them. Eating food filled the belly, but eating sky filled the heart. Asi thought that if she ate enough sky, her skin and hair would turn the color of the veda bird. At first, God punished Asi for being selfish and wanting the color only for herself. But when Asi asked for blue for all her people, the water spirit taught her how to dye with the indigo plant, and Asi brought the knowledge back to her village. Once women knew how to give the beautiful blue color to their clothes, God pulled the sky up out of reach. Today, the legend ends, people can no longer eat the sky, but they have the color of indigo to fill their hearts.

You may have encountered indigo in a list of the colors of the rainbow: red, orange, yellow, green, blue, indigo, violet. If you've ever looked at a rainbow and thought something was wrong with you because you couldn't see the indigo, don't worry. When Isaac Newton first discovered that he could use a prism to split white light into its component colors, he named only five colors in the rainbow, and indigo wasn't one of them: red, yellow, green, blue, and violet-purple. Then Newton decided that the world would be more harmonious if sight and sound corresponded exactly. There were seven intervals between the notes in an octave scale in music, so the rainbow should have *seven* colors. He added orange and indigo to bring the total up to the more satisfying number.

At the time Newton put indigo in the rainbow, the dye was a relative newcomer to Europe. Until the sixteenth century, when the spice trade with the East Indies brought substantial quantities of indigo to Europe, Europeans had used a native plant, woad, to produce blue dye. Chemically, the dyestuff in indigo is identical to the dyestuff in woad, but it is ten times more concentrated. When indigo first appeared on European markets, woad dyers were afraid indigo would put them out of business.

In Frankfurt, they called it "the devil's color." Dyers in Nuremburg had to swear an oath that they wouldn't use it. Henry IV of France declared that dyers could be put to death for dyeing with indigo. But not even these edicts prevented indigo from replacing woad.

Less than a hundred years after Newton gave indigo a place in the rainbow, many women in the American colonies had an indigo dye pot out back to dye the family's clothes. During the American Revolution, when paper currency became worthless, people used lumps of the valuable dyestuff as money. In Japan, indigo is called *ai*, and is traditionally used for work clothes and kimonos. Indigo also gave its color to perhaps the most famous work clothes of all: blue jeans.

Indian Yellow *(1735)* 39
An artist's pigment made in Bengal, India, from the urine of cows or buffalos fed on mango leaves. (For the root of Indian, see Indigo, page 68.)

Ink *(1814)* 189
From Greek *énkaustion*, which meant both a technique of painting with colored wax and a reddish-purple ink that Greek and Roman emperors used for their signatures. The root is *enkáein*, "to burn," because the ink was prepared by heating.

Iris Green *(1835)* 87
A pigment made from the juice of irises. The multicolored flowers take their name from the Greek goddess Iris, a messenger of the gods, who appeared as the rainbow; her name comes from a root that means "to bend, curve."

Iron Gray *(1000)*   188

The color of the metal, whose name may well come from a Celtic root. The Celts were leading metalworkers as early as 1000 B.C.E. "Iron" probably comes ultimately from a Sanskrit root, *isirah*, "to be strong, vigorous." However, since meteorites were an early source of iron for tools and weapons, some etymologists connect the word to the Etruscan *aisar*, "god," because meteorites would have seemed like gods descended from the heavens.

Isabella Color *(1601)*   67

A color allegedly named for Queen Isabella of Castille; while in a town under siege by the Moors, the Queen decided to demonstrate her faith in her troops by vowing not to change her undergarments until the Spaniards were victorious. The siege lasted nine months, and the resulting dingy color of the queen's underwear became known as "Isabella Color."

Ivory *(1385)*   6

From Egyptian *ab*, and Coptic *ebou*, both of which mean "elephant." In Hebrew, ivory is *shen-habbīm*, "tooth of the elephant." The shape of the elephant's tusks may have suggested one of the early uses of carved ivory: by the twelfth century B.C.E., the Chinese were making ivory chopsticks.

Ivory Black *(1634)*   191

An artist's pigment made from burned ivory and other bones. Also known as Bone Black.

Ivy *(1902)*   106

From Old English *īfig*, ultimately from a Germanic root that may be related to Latin *ibex*, "mountain goat": both the plant and the animal are climbers.

is for Jade,
Jasmine Yellow,
Jungle Green, Juniper,
and Jet Black

Jet Black *(1450)* 191

Technically speaking, black is not a color, but the absence of all color. While every color absorbs some wavelengths of light and reflects others, black absorbs all visible wavelengths of light and reflects none. Yet in everyday life we think of black as a color, and even speak of shades of black. Many cultures have words for different kinds of black: the Naisoi of the South Pacific use one word for black that is "dark like a forest" and another for black that is the "dark like night." The Navajo have one word for the black of darkness, another for black objects, including coal and jet. In English, we use "jet" to mean the most intense black of all.

Jet is fossilized driftwood, formed when the wood became buried in the mud of the sea floor. The word "jet" entered English from Old French, which arrived in England with William the Conqueror and the Norman invasion of 1066. Normans were Scandinavians who had settled in northern France, where their Germanic language blended with Latin to form Old French. After the Norman invasion of England, French became the official language of the English court; nobles spoke Norman French, while the ordinary folk spoke Anglo-Saxon, or Old English. Over the next hundred years, the two cultures mingled and the languages blended into one: Middle English.

In Old French, "jet" was *jayete* or *jaiet*, but it comes from the Greek *lithos gagatēs*, or "stone of Gagas," the river in Asia Minor where jet was first unearthed. Jet takes a very high polish, which made it popular for jewelry, but unlike other jewelry, jet brooches, rings, and pendants will burn. The Greeks burned jet deliberately, believing that incense made of jet would repel devils. Nicander, a Greek physician of the second century B.C.E., wrote that the fumes of burning jet would cure the black plague. In the eighth century the Venerable Bede, a medieval historian and theologian, wrote that jet, "when heated, drives away serpents." Pliny, the Roman historian of science, reported that certain magicians would place a piece of jet on a red-hot axe and make a wish. If the stone burned away completely, the wish would come true.

Jade *(1892)* 97

The color of the gemstone, from Spanish *piedra de la ijada*, or "stone of the flank," because jade was believed to be a remedy for kidney ailments. Although green is the most familiar color of jade, the stone can be any color from white to black. In China, where the stone has been highly prized for centuries, names for colors of jade included "melon peel," "date skin," "chicken bone," "cow hair," "coarse rice," "mutton fat," "sky-after-the-rain," "frozen-slush-veined-with-clouds," "purple-of-the-veins," "mucus-of-the-nose gray" and "fish belly." The Chinese discovered early that jade's strength made it valuable for axes and other tools, as well as for religious objects and musical instruments such as chimes. The value of jade made its way into the Chinese language. The Chinese character for "precious" is composed of the ideographs—written symbols that represent objects or ideas rather than sounds—of a house, an earthen jar, a cowrie shell, and jade beads; the ancient ideograph for "ruler" is a string of jade beads. The emperor of China had a jade writing tablet, and perhaps some of the oldest recorded history was found in China, carved in jade.

Jasmine Yellow *(1925)* 3
The color of the flower, from its Persian name, *yāsmīn*.

Jasper Red *(1912)* 25
The color of the stone, from its name in Hebrew, *yāshpeh*, and Akkadian *ashpū*. The stone was valued more in ancient times than it is today; the Roman poet Ovid called it more valuable than gold.

Jonquil Yellow *(1789)*
The color of the flower, from French *jonquille* and ultimately from Latin *iuncus*, "rush, reed," because its leaves resemble reeds.

Jouvence Blue *(1912)* 115
From the French *jouvence*, "youth."

Jungle Green *(1926)* 136
From the Sanskrit *jaṅgala*, "dry ground, desert, waste." A jungle originally meant land that could not be culti-

vated because it was too dry; it came to mean land that could not be cultivated because it was too wet.

Juniper *(1919)* 135

From the Latin name for the tree, *iuniperus*, which may be related to *iuncus*, "reed" (see also Jonquil Yellow, page 74). A wild hare that is being hunted will seek refuge under a juniper tree because the tree's strong scent will hide the hare even from keen-nosed hounds. Another version of the tree's name, *geneva*, or *ginever*, became the name of an aromatic liquor made from the tree's berries: gin.

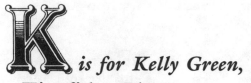

K is for Kelly Green, Kingfisher Blue, and Khaki

Khaki *(1848)*

On New Year's Eve, 1600, Queen Elizabeth I signed the charter of the East India Company. From that moment on, a steady stream of Englishmen set out to make their fortunes in India. The first to arrive were merchants who depended on the protection of the Persian-speaking Mughal rulers of India. Over time, the British effectively became the rulers of the country, and even had their own army of Indian soldiers, known as sepoys.

In 1846 Harry Lumsden, the founding officer of the Corps of Guides in India, wrote to his father, "I am to have the making of this new regiment all to myself. The arming and dressing is to be according to my own fancy." Traditionally, the color of an army's uniforms depended on the leading dye industry of the country. When woad or indigo was the main dye, the uniforms were blue, as in Prussia. When madder was the principal dyestuff, the uniforms were red. France started out with blue uniforms, until the local madder industry needed a boost; then Louis Philippe declared that French uniforms should be red. During the American Civil War, the Confederate army dyed its uniforms with what it had on hand: the husks of butternuts, a type of walnut. The troops became known as "butternuts."

Lumsden rejected a uniform proposed by his second-in-command as "too flash for Guides." Instead, his "fancy" was to take his sepoys out of the traditional British "redcoat," dyed with madder, and substitute a uniform more suited to the sultry Indian climate: loose shirts and pantaloons. For the color of this unlikely uniform, he wanted something that would make his soldiers disappear into the landscape. He chose khaki, whose name comes from Hindi, the language of Northern India and a distant cousin of English in the vast Indo-European family of languages. Hindi has both Arabic and Persian roots; in Persian, the ancestor of Farsi, the language of modern Iran, *khāk* meant "earth, or dust," and in Hindi, *khākī* meant "dusty, or dust-colored." Lumsden himself called the cloth "mud-colour." In 1849, when the Guides were on an expedition with regularly uniformed British soldiers, a member of the artillery mistook the khaki-clad Guides for the enemy and was about to fire when another soldier called out, "Lord, Sir, them is our mudlarks!"

Lumsden was quite proud of his troops' uniforms; to the coat, pantaloons, and greatcoat, he added deerskin gaiters to cover the calves. He proclaimed that the Guides would be "the most smashing regiment in India." When Lumsden took one of his officers to meet "the Old Gentleman," Sir Charles Napier, Commander-in-Chief in India, Sir Charles looked them up and down and gave his grudging approval. "Yes, it's not a bad color for work." If that seems a little cool, the Old Gentleman later remarked that the Guides were the "only properly dressed Riflemen in India."

Other British soldiers did not wear khaki until the Great Indian Mutiny a decade later. The British had taken control of India without much respect for local religions or customs. Indian anger at the British attitude reached the boiling point in 1857, when a new shipment of ammunition required sepoys to bite off the end of the cartridges in order to load their rifles. Rumors flew that the cartridges had been greased with a mixture of lard (pork fat) and suet (beef fat). To the Muslim sepoys, pork was an unclean, forbidden food; Hindu sepoys, on the other hand, held the cow to be sacred, and therefore not to be eaten. Everyone was insulted, and the long and bloody Indian Mutiny was under way.

British troops fighting the sepoys quickly realized that dusty, khaki-colored uniforms would hide them from snipers' bullets. Soldiers brought white cloth to the local bazaar to be dyed, and local merchants used whatever was available: mud, tea leaves, coffee, even a mixture of red and black office inks. In these early days, "khaki" was not a standard color, but whatever emerged from the bazaar, ranging from off-white to slate to lavender to brown. European observers refused to believe that these mismatched, turbaned soldiers, whose belted flannel shirts were not even tucked into their trousers, could be an English army. It took some time for the English themselves to become accustomed to the new uniform. In the next few hot-weather campaigns, the army was allowed to travel in khaki, but had to put its regulation uniform back on when it came time to fight.

Kelly Green *(1936)* 86

From Kelly, a common Irish surname. The color name was inspired by the popular song "Has Anybody Here

Seen Kelly?" Ireland, the "Emerald Isle," also gave rise to the color name Killarney Green (1912), which takes its name from a town in Ireland.

Kingfisher Blue *(1919)*

The color of the bird's plumage; the bird's name comes from its crownlike tuft of feathers and its habit of diving for fish and sea animals. In legend, the kingfisher was originally a gray bird that got its color by fleeing Noah's ark in such a hurry that it rubbed against the sky. The kingfisher was traditionally associated with the fabled halcyon, whose name comes from Greek *háls*, "sea," and *kuôn*, "conceive," because the bird was said to build a nest stronger than iron on the surface of the water. For four weeks in midwinter, the gods would calm the waves while the birds nested and fed their young. Hence, "halcyon days" are a time of peace and tranquility. In German the kingfisher is *eisvogel*, or "steel bird." The German name for the color is *eisblau*, which entered English, in a translation based on sound rather than meaning, as Ice Blue (1933).

*is for Lacquer Red,
Lampblack, Leek Green,
Lobster Red,
and Lavender*

Lavender *(1858)*   (Lavender Blue *(1796)*) 158

Lavender is a flower in the mint family whose name comes from the Latin *lavare*, "to wash," the same root as our word laundry. The ancient Romans used lavender to scent their wash water, and ever since then, people have used the flower to perfume both themselves and their linens.

Romans accustomed to using lavender in their baths probably introduced the plant to England. The first Romans arrived on British soil in 54 B.C.E. with Julius Caesar. Eleven years later, under the emperor Claudius, Romans invaded in force. Within one hundred years, they had taken over the island, bringing their Latin language with them. In the year 410, the Romans withdrew to deal with pressing problems back at home.

The Latin language (and some Greek) returned to Britain three hundred years later with the first Christian missionaries, who came to convert the Angles, Saxons, and Jutes, the Germanic tribes who had taken over the island. A mixture of their languages had formed Old English, which now got an infusion of Latin and Greek from the monasteries, where monks used the classical languages to teach poetry, arithmetic, and astronomy as well as religion. In 1066, the Norman invasion brought legal Latin to England. During the Renaissance, Latin was the international language of science and philosophy.

Like Latin, lavender flourished in England. In London, you can find a Lavender Street, Lavender Hill, Lavender Lane, and Lavender Sweep. During outbreaks of plague and other diseases, people would strew lavender on the floors of houses and churches both to cover up odors and to ward off disease. Its strong scent made people sneeze, making it a valuable ingredient in snuff and in smelling salts, which were used to revive people who had fainted (often women whose corsets were laced too tightly). Queen Victoria was particularly partial to lavender. One observer wrote that the "royal residences are strongly impregnated with the refreshing odour of this old-fashioned flower, and there is no perfume that the Queen likes better than lavender-water, which, together with the oil for disinfecting purposes, Her Majesty has direct from a lady who distils it herself."

In the seventeenth century, people would say "lavender blue" or "lavender gray," meaning the blue of fresh lavender blossoms or the gray of the dried herb, just as we might say "rose red" or "dandelion yellow." People even said "lavender green," meaning the color of the leaves and stems of the lavender plant. A ballad first published around 1680 contained the verse, "Lavender's blue, dilly, dilly/ Lavender's green,/When I am king, dilly, dilly,/ You shall be queen." By the nineteenth century, "lavender" had come to stand on its own as a color name.

Lacquer Red *(1925)* 60

From French *lacre*, "sealing wax." Lacquer is a glossy resin, applied in layers to build up shine and color. Ultimately the name comes from "lac," a dyestuff and ingredient of shellac that comes from the secretion of the *Coccus lacca* insect, whose name in turn comes from the Hindi *lākh*, "one hundred thousand," because of the huge number of insects that cover a single plant.

Lampblack *(1598)* 191

An artist's pigment, almost pure carbon, made by condensing the smoke of burning oil, tar, pitch, or resin. "Lamp" comes from Greek *lampein*, "to shine." In China, 3,500 years ago, lampblack was obtained by lighting several hundred oil lamps at once in an area enclosed by bamboo and removing the soot every half hour with a feather.

Lead Gray *(1705)* 188

Lead comes to English through Celtic, ultimately from an Indo-European root that means "to flow," as the metal does when heated. The color is also known as Plumbago Grey (1912). Plumbago was the name given to a form of carbon, also known as graphite (see page 61). *Plumbago* is also the Latin word for lead ore, which explains why the symbol for lead on the periodic table is Pb, and why a person who works with (lead) pipe is a plumber.

Leaf Green *(1891)* 85

Middle English *leef*, from an Indo-European root that means "to strip, to peel," which originally referred to bark, but eventually came to mean foliage in general.

Leek Green (1662) 88

The color of the vegetable, from its Old English name *lēac*, which meant "leek, onion, garlic." This root is also the source of the "lic" in "garlic" and the "lock" in "hemlock," and may be related to *lūcan*, "to weed, to pull up." The Roman emperor Nero used to eat raw leeks several days a month to clear his voice; his nickname was "Leek-eater."

Lemon Yellow (1598) 1

The color of the fruit, from its Persian name, *līmūn*. Lemons turn yellow only when they are exposed to cold. The cold breaks down the chlorophyll, or green pigment, leaving the carotenoids, or yellow pigments, visible. In the seventeenth century, people started using lemon juice as invisible ink: when heated, the ink becomes visible.

Lettuce Green (1884) 95

From French *laitue*, "lettuce," and ultimately from Latin *lactuca*, "milky," because of the milky juice, or latex, that the older plants exude when you cut them. Early Romans ate lettuce at the very end of the meal because they thought it would make them sleepy, and in fact the latex, particularly of wild lettuces, does contain a sleep-inducing chemical not unlike opium.

Lichen Green (1898) 98

A lichen is not really a plant but a combination of an alga and a fungus. The alga does not have a way to obtain water; the fungus cannot make its own food, so the fungus absorbs water and gives it to the alga; the alga uses the water, together with sunlight, to make food, which it shares with the fungus. Together, they form a lichen, whose name comes from the Greek *leikhein*, "to lick," because of the way lichens cover rocks and trees. Some lichens are potent dyes; others can be used to make bread, and some people even speculate that these lichens could have been the manna dropped from heaven for the Israelites in the wilderness mentioned in the Book of Exodus.

Licorice Black *(n.d.)* 191
The color of candy flavored with licorice, whose name comes from Greek *glyccorhiza*, or "sweet root."

Lilac *(1775)* 160
From Arabic *laylak* and Persian *nīlak*, a diminutive of *nil*, "blue." Lilacs became so popular in the nineteenth century that one Paris hothouse employed eighty men and eighty strong horses just to cultivate them.

Lily White *(1310)* 123
The color of the flower, from its Latin name, *līlium*, which comes from Greek *leirion*, and ultimately perhaps from Coptic *hrēri* or *hlēli*.

Lime Green *(1905)* 91
From Arabic *līma*, probably from the Persian *līmūn*, "lemon." In the fourteenth century, Sir John Maundeville reported that inhabitants of Ceylon (now Sri Lanka) found limes to have miraculous powers. In one lake in Ceylon he "found many precious stones and great pearls." Once a year, according to Maundeville, the king allowed the poor to dive for the precious gems. However, the lake was also home to "many cockodrills [crocodiles] and serpents and great water leeches." To protect themselves from the beasts, the divers covered

"their arms, thighs, and legs with an ointment made of a thing called limons, which is a kind of fruit like small pease, and then they have no dread of cockodrills, or other venomous things."

Liver *(1686)* 73

Old English *lifer*, from an Indo-European root that means "to stick, adhere, to be fat." The liver was the fatty organ; it was also believed to be the organ that produced blood, and so caused people to stick around, to live.

Lobster Red *(1789)* 26

From Latin *locusta*, "locust, flying creature," which the lobster resembles, possibly combined with Old English *loppe*, "spider." Carotene pigments give cooked lobsters their bright color; in a live lobster, the carotene is hidden in a bond with a protein, but the heat of cooking breaks those bonds and reveals the carotene's true colors. Although lobster is now an expensive food, lobsters were so plentiful when Europeans first arrived in America that they often provided food for the poor. The settlers didn't even have to set traps: lobsters washed up on the beaches, sometimes in piles several feet high. And while today's lobsters may weigh only one or two pounds, a single lobster then could weigh more than forty. During the American Revolution, lobsters fled New York harbor, disturbed by the bombardment of ships, but they returned when the war was over.

Loden Green *(1916)* 105

The characteristic color of a type of heavy wool cloth, from Old High German *lodo*, "coarse cloth."

is for Madder Red, Mauve, Mocha, Mummy Brown, and Magenta

Magenta *(1860)* 15

The year was 1859. The land we know as Italy was a patchwork of kingdoms, duchies, and Papal states. Austria ruled the northern provinces of Lombardy and Venetia. In neighboring France, Louis Napoleon, the nephew of Napoleon Bonaparte, had declared himself Emperor Napoleon III, and was looking for a way to turn France into a power in international affairs. As a boy visiting his relatives, the young Louis Napoleon had seen the sufferings of the Italians under Austrian rule. His beloved brother had died in a rebellion in Italy. Napoleon III thought he could add to the glory of France by helping the Italians turn the Austrians out of their country.

The Franco-Italian army first met the Austrians in battle on June 4, in a Lombard town that had been the *castra Maxentia,* or camp of the emperor Maxentius, in the early fourth century. (In England, place names that end in "chester" or "caster" or "cester," all versions of *castra,* are similar evidence of former Roman settlements.) Over time, Italians had dropped the *castra* and *Maxentia* had slurred into "Magenta."

The Battle of Magenta was followed on June 24 by the Battle of Solferino. Both battles were extremely bloody, with many thousands dead on both sides. One observer of the Battle of Solferino, a Swiss philanthropist named Jean-Henri Dunant, was so shocked by the carnage that he went on to found the International Red Cross, whose mission was to help the wounded on the field of battle, whatever their nationality. The French losses at Magenta and Solferino were enormous, and the victories narrow, but they were enough to spark the nationalist movement that led to the unification of Italy in 1861.

Back in France, chemists were beginning to experiment with the new aniline dyes, which had been invented in England only two years earlier by an eighteen-year-old chemistry student, William Henry Perkin. Perkin hadn't set out to make dyes at all. In a home laboratory he'd built so that he could experiment during his school vacations, Perkin was trying to use coal tar to synthesize quinine, the cure for malaria. At first Perkin got only an ugly black sludge, but when his experiments produced some purple crystals, he thought he'd try to dye silk with them. It worked. With some help from his father and brother, Perkin started manufacturing the dye in his back garden. He called the new color "Tyrian Purple" or "Perkin's Violet." Perkin's dye business was so successful that he was later knighted, and retired at the grand old age of thirty-five.

In 1859, following Perkin's example, a French chemist named Verguin invented a similar dye. He named it magenta in honor of his emperor's recent victory. (Some people called the new color fuchsine, after the fuchsia flower.) A purple dye named solferino was also quite popular in the nineteenth century, but has long since gone out of fashion. The city of Paris named a street after Solferino, and another after Magenta, on which stood the house of the Impressionist painter Georges Seurat, who was born in the year of the Battle of Magenta and became famous for his *pointilliste* style of creating images out of tiny areas of color.

Madder Red *(1727)* 25
From Old English *maeddere*, which comes from Sanskrit *madhura*, "sweet, tender." Madder is one of the oldest known red dyes (see page 15); it will even dye the beaks and claws of birds and the bones and teeth of animals who feed on it. If an animal alternates between eating grass and madder root, its bones will be dyed in concentric circles of red, like the rings of a tree. As an artist's pigment, it is known as Rose Madder (1807).

Mahogany *(1737)* 78
The color of the wood, perhaps from a Mayan language of Honduras, or the Arawak language of the West Indies.

Maize *(1838)* 62
The color of corn, from the language of the Taino or Arawak people of Haiti, *mahiz*, "life-giver." Maize has been cultivated in Mexico and Central America for five thousand years, although the earliest varieties were probably closer to the corn we use for popcorn than to the corn on the cob we eat today. Maize was central to the mythology of many of the peoples of the region. In one legend of the Aztecs, the last great empire of Mexico, the first man and woman told their future by tossing kernels of maize. Although corn comes in many colors, including white, black, blue, red, and orange, the yellow

color we associate with corn comes from the pigment xanthophyll (Greek for "yellow leaf") and gives the skin and legs of corn-fed chickens a yellow color.

Malachite Green *(1880)*   134
The color of the stone, a copper carbonate. The name comes from the Greek *malakhē*, or "mallow plant," whose leaves the stone resembles (see Mauve, page 90). Egyptians used ground malachite as a paint and as an eyeshadow, surrounding the eye to protect it from glare, much like the under-eye smudges of today's athletes.

Mandarin Orange *(1883)*   40
The color of the fruit, which takes its name from the color of the robes of the Chinese officials known as mandarins, from the Sanskrit *mantrin*, "counselor."

Manganese Violet *(1902)*   168
An artist's pigment made from the element manganese, named for Magnesia, in Thessaly, which also gave its name to the magnet.

Marigold *(1654)*   39
The color of the flower, originally simply called *golde*, but in the Middle Ages renamed "Mary's gold." In Gaelic, it is *lusmairi* or "Mary's leek." Marigolds have been used to color butter and cheese, as well as to dye cloth and hair. William Turner, a sixteenth-century naturalist, grumbled, "Some use to make their heyre yellow wyth the flowre of this herbe, not beying content with the natural colour, which God hath given them."

Maroon *(1789)*   34
From French *marron* and Italian *marrone*, "chestnut."

Mars Yellow *(1835)* 39
An artist's pigment whose color comes from iron oxide; "Mars," the Roman god of war, is an old name for iron, the metal from which many weapons of war were made.

Massicot Yellow *(1472)* 6
A painter's pigment made from lead oxide. The name may go back to the Spanish *mazacote*, mortar.

Mauve *(1856)* 167
The color of the flowers of the mallow plant (see Malachite Green, page 89), called *mauve* in French, which in turn comes from Latin *malva*, or "soft," describing the texture of the mallow's leaves. In France, Perkin's Violet (see page 87), the first aniline dye, became known as "mauve." In 1862, Queen Victoria set the fashion in England by wearing a mauve dress to the Great Exhibition; the humor magazine *Punch* showed a London policeman telling traffic to "Get a mauve on!"

Melon *(1892)* 21
The color of the fruit, from Greek *mēlon*, which meant "apple," but was also used for fruit generally. Usually the color of canteloupe, whose name comes from Cantelupo in Italy, the Pope's summer estate, where the melons were grown.

Midnight Blue *(1915)* 154
"Mid" comes from an Indo-European root that means "the middle"; "night" from Old English *niht*, "night."

Milk White *(1000)* 6
From Old English *milc*, from an Indo-European root that means "to wipe, to stroke, to press out," and came to mean "to milk."

Mimosa *(1909)*   5

The color of the flower, whose name comes from the Greek *mimeisthai*, "to imitate," because some species appear to imitate animal life by folding their leaves when touched.

Mint Green *(1920)*   125

From the Greek name for the plant, *minthē*. In Greek legend, Hades, the god of the underworld, fell in love with a nymph named Minthe. Before he could carry her off, his wife, Persephone, intervened and turned Minthe into the plant that now bears her name.

Mocha *(1895)*   82

The name of a port city in Yemen from which coffee was shipped; the town gave its name to a kind of coffee, and then to a mixture of coffee and chocolate.

Moss Green *(1884)*   108

From Old English *mos*, "marsh, moor, bog." A related word in Old High German also means "mildew, lichen, moss." Both come from an Indo-European root that means "moist."

Mouse Gray *(1606)*   70

From Old English *mūs*, from an Indo-European root that means "to steal," because the mouse is "the stealing animal." The root gives us both "mouse" and "muscle," because the movements of a muscle resemble a darting mouse.

Mulberry *(1776)*   176

From Latin *mōrum*, "mulberry, blackberry," from a root that means "to be black"; and Old High German *beri*, "berry." Pliny, the Roman natural historian, called the mulberry the wisest of trees because it was the last to unfurl its leaves and so was least affected by the cold weather; he also said that once the leaves were out, the mulberry grew so fast you could hear the buds opening. In the Middle Ages, mulberries were used as a dye both for food and for illuminated manuscripts. In the seventeenth century, mulberries were used to dye cider so that unscrupulous merchants could pass it off as wine.

Mummy Brown *(1886)*   (Mummy *(1598)*) 110
An artist's pigment, supposed to have been made from the remains of Egyptian mummies. From Arabic *mūmiyah*, "preserved body," ultimately from Persian *mūm*, "wax."

Mushroom *(1892)*   111
From French *mousseron*, probably meaning "little moss."

Mustard *(1848)*   64
The color of the seasoning, which comes from the Latin *mustum*, "new, fresh." "Must" came to mean freshly fermenting grape juice, an ingredient in the earliest mustard; the suffix "ard" comes from a Teutonic root meaning "hard," referring to the mustard's bite. In this case, the plant and seed took their name from the seasoning, and not the other way around.

Myrtle Green *(1835)*   117
From a Semitic root meaning "to be bitter," the same root as the fragrant myrrh. In Greek myth, Aphrodite wore a crown of myrtle sprigs when she rose from the sea. Romans wore crowns of myrtle after a victory in battle, but only if none of their side's blood had been shed.

is for Naples Yellow,
National School Bus Chrome Yellow,
Nile Green, Nutmeg, and
Nasturtium Yellow

Nasturtium Yellow _(1845)_   39

Nasturtium is a flower whose name comes from the
Latin _nasus_, meaning "nose," and _torquere_, meaning
"to twist." (The same root gives us the word "tor-
ture.") In ancient times, nasturtium, the nose-twisting
or nose-tormenting plant, meant watercress. In the sixteenth century, the English borrowed the name for a
plant recently imported from Peru, which they also
called Indian cress. Neither the Latin nor the English
name, "nose-smart," referred to the plant's scent, but
rather to the stinging sensation in your nose when you
ate it. Like watercress, nasturtiums are edible, with a
sweet nectar in the flower's long spur and plenty of vitamin C in the peppery leaves.

Unlike most other animals, humans don't produce
their own vitamin C, and need to get it from their food.
Lack of vitamin C causes scurvy, a disease that makes
you bleed beneath the skin and causes your teeth and
bones to become brittle and your hair to fall out.

Scurvy, which can be fatal, was a particular danger to sailors, who had to travel on long voyages without fresh fruits or vegetables. Until the end of the eighteenth century, people ate nasturtium leaves to prevent scurvy.

In 1762, nineteen-year-old Elisabet Christina Linnaea published a scientific paper about nasturtiums, which, she said, were becoming so popular "on account of their brilliant flowers" that they "will soon be in every cabbage patch and . . . soon every child will know them." Elisabet Christina's family had planted nasturtiums near an arbor in their garden. While sitting in the arbor at dusk on a summer evening, Elisabet Christina saw the nasturtium flower "shimmer very thickly." (Elisabet Christina was apparently fond of experimenting in the family garden. She had discovered that the air around the oil glands of the dittany plant was flammable—hence dittany's other name, "candle plant"—and liked to set it on fire.) She showed her discovery about nasturtiums to other people, who also saw the "hasty flash of brilliance" and were "delighted by it." Arriving home after a week's absence, her father, Carolus Linnaeus, the Swedish botanist who developed the system of classifying plants we still use today, was dubious about his daughter's observation, "even though," she said, "I brought forward many witnesses who had seen it with me." But on the following evening, he had to admit his daughter was right.

Scientists puzzled over Elisabet Christina's observation. Alessandro Volta, the Italian scientist and inventor of the battery, thought the nasturtium's sparks were electrical. A British botanist suggested that the plants might be using electricity to defend themselves against night-flying insects. The German poet and philosopher Johann Wolfgang von Goethe dismissed what she had seen as an optical illusion called an afterimage, which is produced by staring for a long time at a brightly colored object. When you look away from the object at a white surface, the color receptors in your eye that normally register the color you've been staring at are tired, and so you see white light *minus* that color. After staring at the yellow-orange nasturtium, said Goethe, you naturally see a brief bluish glow.

In June 1889, a British cleric named Russel not only saw the sparks, he also saw the nasturtium's leaves glowing even after he took them indoors into a darkened room. Russel described what he saw when he examined a leaf under a microscope. "The appearance of the luminous vapour floating over its surface (like moonlight on rippling water) was strikingly beautiful," he wrote. "The whole leaf seemed to twinkle with points of light—the main ribs, radiating from a common centre, shining out like a silver star."

Today, scientists attribute the sparks and glowing leaves to the plant's high content of phosphoric acid.

Nacarat *(1727)*   26
From the Spanish, *nacardo*, "mother-of-pearl," ultimately from Arabic *naqqāra*, "a drum," describing the shape of the hollow shell from which mother-of-pearl comes. Nacarat may also be related to the Arabic *naka'at*, a red flower used as a dye. A dye called nacarat was made from goat's hair that had soaked in madder for three days. (See Madder Red, page 88.)

Naples Yellow *(1738)*   36
An artist's pigment made from the element antimony, whose name probably comes, via Arabic, from Egyptian *sdm*, a powder used to decorate the eyes. In the Middle Ages, alchemists used antimony, and the idea sprung up that its name came from the French *anti-moine*, or

"against the monks." Naples Yellow was named for the Italian city where the pigment was used in the Middle Ages and was known as *giallolino di fornace* or "oven yellow."

National School Bus Chrome Yellow *(1950)* 37

In the United States, the standard color for school buses, because of its high visibility. The color was designated by the General Services Administration in 1950, and recommended for national use by the Occupational Safety and Health Administration in 1971. Chrome Yellow is a painter's pigment invented in 1797 from the element chrome, which takes its name from Greek *chroma*, "color," because of the brilliant colors that occur in its compounds.

Natural *(1928)* 49

The color of undyed cloth. From Latin *natura*, "nature," and ultimately from *nasci*, "to be born," because what is natural is what a living being is born with.

Navy *(1840)* 151

The color of the British naval uniform, which was dyed with indigo (see page 68). Naval officers began wearing blue in the eighteenth century by order of King George II, who was inspired by the blue-and-white riding habit of the Duchess of Bedford; blue became the official color for all sailors by order of Parliament in 1857. "Navy" comes from Latin *navigare*, "to sail."

Nectarine *(1899)* 20

The color of the fruit, named for the Greek *nektar*, the food of the gods, either from Indo-European roots that mean "death" and "victorious," because nectar made the gods immortal; or from Hebrew *yayin niqtar*, "smoked or perfumed wine."

Nickel Green *(1912)* 127
The element nickel gets its name from German *kupfernickel*, "copper devil," because the gleaming ore looked as though it might yield copper but did not.

Nile Blue *(1873)* 119
Nile Green *(1888)* 126
The colors of the African river, often considered the longest in the world; according to Egyptian legend, the Nile flooded because of the tears of the goddess Isis. Some etymologists trace the Persian word *nil* (see page 84) to the Nile, and say that both words originally meant "black": the Nile was the Black River.

Nut Brown *(1300)* 80
From Old English *hnutu*, "nut," from an Indo-European root meaning "lump."

Nutmeg *(1610)* 71
The color of the spice, from Latin, *nux*, "nut," and Provençal *muscat*, "musky." The aroma of the tree is said to intoxicate birds of paradise, and indeed, too much nutmeg can cause people to hallucinate.

**is for Oak,
Oatmeal, Olive, Orchid,
and Oxblood Red**

Oxblood Red *(1705)*   30

"Red" is one of the oldest color words in English, going back to an Indo-European root, *rhudirá*, that means "blood." The same root also gives us "ruddy" and the color name "rust" (see page 123). Although the ancients didn't know it, both the color of blood and the color of rust come from the interaction of iron and oxygen. The red blood cells of all vertebrates contain the pigment hemoglobin, a protein that contains iron and bonds easily with oxygen, giving blood its characteristic red color. When we say "blood red," we really mean arterial blood, which carries oxygen throughout the body, rather than venous blood, which, having delivered its oxygen is much bluer. When exposed to oxygen in air, it immediately turns red, so people bleed red no matter where they are cut.

The association of red and blood is almost universal. In many languages the two words are identical, or closely related. The Aleuts, for example, call red *aukpaluktak*, from *auk*, meaning "blood," and *paluqpoq*, "resembles." When speaking to people who aren't fluent in their language, they simply use *auk* for "red." Some cultures form color names by repeating the name of an object of that color; "red" is often "bloodblood." For example, among one people of New Guinea, *mep* means "blood," and *mepmep* means "red."

Although "red" originally meant "blood," the English word "blood" does not come from the same root. The Anglo-Saxons probably had a word for blood that looked something like the Sanskrit *rhudira*. But at some very early point in the evolution of English, people became superstitious about using that word, or the Latin word for blood, *sanguinis*. This *rhudira* or *sanguinis* was the life force; if you lost too much of it, you would die. Words had mysterious, magical power: to speak the name of this powerful substance out loud might put a person's very life in danger. So instead, Anglo-Saxon speakers created a new word—a code word—"blood," from the root "to bloom" or "to blossom," a poetic way of describing the way the vital red liquid welled up from a wound.

In English, "blood red" has been a color name since the thirteenth century. Since the blood of all mammals is pretty much the same color, why bother to name a separate color *ox*blood red? "Ox," by the way, comes from an ancient Indo-European root that means "male animal," or "the besprinkler," and is related to the Welsh and Old Irish words for "stag": *ych* and *oss*. The plural, "oxen," is a vestige of the period of Middle English during which the North of England favored plurals ending in *s* or *es*, and the South favored *en*. The North won out, but a few Southern plurals survived: we still say "oxen" and "children," and have a choice between saying "brethren" and "brothers."

In the eighteenth century, when "oxblood" entered the language as a color name, people were much more familiar with the color of oxblood than we are today. Many cultures took blood directly from live animals to use as food; as late as the eighteenth century, the blood of oxen and other cattle was an ingredient in cooking in both Scotland and Ireland.

The idea of calling a color oxblood may have come from the dye industry. Dyers actually used oxblood, supplied by butchers, as an ingredient in the complicated recipe for the prized color known as Turkey red. Although blood actually turns black when heated during the dyeing process, both the dyers and their customers may have attributed the intense color of Turkey red to the oxblood rather than to its real source, madder root. Curiously, in 1704, oxblood was one of the ingredients in the first man-made pigment. A German dyer named Diesbach was attempting to produce a red dye, but what he got was a color that takes its name from Diesbach's homeland: Prussian Blue (1724).

Oxblood may originally have meant the bright color of fresh blood, but it has come to mean a shade of Chinese pottery and dyed leather closer to the color of dried blood. Jewelers use "oxblood" to describe a color of opals, and "pigeon's blood" for the color of particularly fine rubies. ("Ruby," incidentally, goes back to the same Indo-European root as "red.") Other "blood" reds include "dragon's blood," which, according to Pliny, is the only pigment that properly represents blood in painting. Dragon's blood is actually the resin of a palm tree, but Pliny insisted it was "the gore of a dragon crushed beneath the weight of dying elephants," the two bloods mingling in a single stream.

Oak *(1888)* 51
From Old English *āc*, "oak," similar to Latin *aesculus*,

"oak sacred to Jupiter." Oaks were also sacred to the Druids of Britain, who did not believe in worshiping their gods indoors. Their holy sites were outside, often near groves of oak; they held all their criminal trials under oak trees.

Oatmeal *(1927)*   68
From Anglo-Saxon *āte*, "oats," which may be related to Norwegian *eitel*, "knot, nodule," and Russian *iadro*, "kernel, bullet, ball, shot," all of which come from a root that means "to swell." *Melo*, "meal," is ultimately from Latin *molina*, "mill": meal is grain that has been milled.

Ochre *(1398)*   62
See page 153.

Olive *(1613)*   104
The color of the green fruit. From the Greek *elaia*, "oil," related to Armenian *eul*, "oil," both probably from an older Cretan source. The green olives we associate with the color are actually unripe; a ripening olive will turn violet, then dark purple, then black. Sometimes green olives are served stuffed with Pimento (1921), a sweet red pepper whose name comes from Latin *pigmenta*, meaning "vegetable juices, condiments, pigments," from *pingere*, "to paint."

Orange *(1512)*   54
See page 150.

Orchid *(1915)*   163
The color of one pale variety of the flower, whose name comes from the Greek *orkhis*, meaning "testicle," refer-

101

ring to the shape of the flower's bulbs. Part of orchids' popularity may be that they are long lasting. Orchids often live as much as 360 feet off the ground on the bark of tropical trees. The blossoms stay open because it may take weeks for the fertilizing insect they need to reach them. Orchid collecting became a passion in nineteenth-century England. Orchid hunters would compete with one another to bring back ever-rarer specimens from tropical lands, and would try to outwit one another by leaving false maps and trails for their competition to find. One such adventurer, known as the King of the Orchid Hunters, lost a hand in pursuit of the flowers and had to continue his work with an iron hook in its place. Perhaps to avoid such mishaps, one twentieth-century botanist taught a berok monkey named Merah to gather orchids. The monkey, on a leash, would climb up a tree and eat a meal of mangoes or coconuts. Then Merah, who understood 18 words of Malay, would listen for instructions about which orchids to gather.

Orpiment *(1386)* 4
An artist's pigment, also known as King's Yellow. Its name comes from Latin *auripigmentum*, "gold color." Orpiment is highly poisonous; the fifteenth-century artist Cennino Cennini advised painters, "Beware of letting it soil your mouth, lest you harm yourself."

Otter *(1880)* 80
The color of the animal's pelt. Its name comes from an Indo-European root that means "water": the otter is "the water animal." The Spanish word for otter, Nutria (1892), also became a color name.

Oyster White *(1893)*

The color of the inside of an oyster shell; from Greek *ostreon*, "oyster," ultimately from an Indo-European root that means "bone," and is related to Greek *ostakos*, "crustacean," and *ostrakon*, "hard shell, piece of broken pottery."

**is for Pansy,
Peach, Pink, Plum,
and Persimmon**

Persimmon *(1919)*

When English-speaking explorers first traveled to new
lands, they often encountered plants and animals they
had never seen before. Even when they changed the
name of the land itself, as they did in Virginia, naming
it after Elizabeth I, the Virgin Queen, the English
tended to borrow the local names for plants and animals
rather than making up ones of their own. In Virginia,
the local language was Powhatan, a member of the Algonquian family of languages. Algonquian people in-
habited the eastern portion of North America from
what is now Labrador in Canada all the way to the Car-
olinas. Among the unfamiliar sights of Virginia was a
strange fruit, whose name in Powhatan was *putchamin*
or *pasiminan*, meaning "dried fruit." In English, the
Algonquian name became "persimmon."

The English visitors tried to describe this new fruit to
friends and relatives back home. Captain John Smith explained that the Powhatans preserved the fruit "like
Pruines." A traveler named Strachey said it was "like to

a medler, in England, but a deeper tawnie cullour." (A "medler," or medlar, is a European fruit similar to an apple.) In 1585, Thomas Hariot, astronomer and mathematics tutor to Sir Walter Raleigh, said persimmons were "as red as cheries and very sweet: but whereas the cherie is sharpe sweet, they are lushious sweet." Hariot remarked that persimmons were "not good until they were rotten." He was one of the lucky ones who tasted persimmons after the first frost; before the frost, explained someone who had learned the hard way, "they are harsh and choakie, and furre in a man's mouth." Another sufferer observed that an unripe persimmon "will draw a man's mouth awry with much torment, but when it is ripe, it is as delicious as an Apricock."

So notorious was the effect of an unripe persimmon that the early settlers said that someone with a sour expression must have been "eating a green 'simmon." By the nineteenth century, people must have learned how to eat persimmons properly: one settler in Indiana compared their flavor to "raisins dipped in honey"; and to "walk off with the persimmons" meant to win the prize. Settlers made sweet syrup and table beer from the fruit, and even roasted and ground the seeds when coffee was scarce. Indeed, persimmons were considered a dish fit for royalty: in 1872, when the Fifth Avenue Hotel in Topeka, Kansas, prepared a feast of 107 dishes for the Grand Duke Alexis of Russia, the menu included roast opossum (another Powhatan word) with persimmon jelly.

Palomino *(1914)*   41
A color of horses, from the American Spanish *paloma*, "dove," referring to the horse's grayish-yellow coat.

Pansy *(1705)*   155
The color of the flower, whose name comes from the

French *pensée*, "thought," which comes from Latin *pensare*, "to weigh, ponder, consider." Giving someone a pansy was supposed to keep you in his or her thoughts. Gerard, author of one of the first herbals, was very fond of pansies. "Gardens themselves receive by these the greatest ornament of all," he wrote, "chiefest beauty and most gallant grace."

Paprika *(1921)*   60
The color of the spice, from Hungarian *paprika*, ultimately from Serbo-Croatian *pàpar*, "pepper." In some cases, paprika acts as a dye: if a canary eats too much paprika, its feathers will turn red.

Parma Violet *(1941)*   178
The color of the flower, named for the town of Parma, Italy. This variety is much prized by gardeners. The English poet Walter Savage Landor cultivated them; once, in a fit of temper, he threw his cook out of the window, only then remembering what was planted below: "Good God!" he cried. "I forgot the violets!"

Parrot Green *(1646)*   90
After the plumage of the bird, whose name comes from the French *Perrot*, a diminutive of Peter. The color was also known as Gay Green (1837), from the Greek for "parrot," *papagás* (the last syllable, *gas*, became "gay"), which may in turn come from Arabic *babaghā*, an onomatopoetic, or imitative, word for the bird's call.

Pastel Blue *(1789)*   147
From the French name for the dyeplant woad, *pastel*, ultimately from a Latin root meaning "paste," because dyers had to crush the plant into a paste to use it. Ancient Britons used woad to dye themselves blue before

going into battle. This was supposed to make them look ghostly and fierce, but the smell may have been a weapon as well: the stench of fermenting woad was so offensive that Queen Elizabeth I forbade any woad dyeing within five miles of any of her country residences.

Payne's Gray (1835)   143
A watercolor pigment, named for the early nineteenth-century English artist William Payne.

Pea Green (1752)   94
The color of the vegetable; from Greek *pison*, from a root that means "to grind, to pound." In Middle English the singular was "pease," but this sounded like a plural, and people invented "pea" as the singular. In Scandinavian countries, the pea is sacred to Thor. According to legend, Thor was so angry at humankind that he sent a slew of dragons to stop up their wells with peas. The dragons carried the peas in their talons, and dropped some of them onto the ground by mistake. Ever since, Scandinavians have traditionally eaten peas on Thor's day—Thursday. Even today the Swedish Army eats pea soup every Thursday. Although green is the color we associate with peas, not all peas are green, a fact that led a nineteenth-century Austrian monk, Gregor Mendel, to conduct one of the earliest genetic experiments. Mendel discovered that if he crossed a yellow pea and a green pea, all of the offspring were green. His observation that some characteristics, like the green color of peas, were dominant, and others, like the yellow, were recessive—was a major contribution to what would become the science of genetics.

Peach (1588)   20
The color of the fruit. From Latin *malum Persicum*,

"Persian apple." Peaches are native to China, where they have been cultivated for four thousand years and are a symbol of immortality. The West did not discover peaches until people carried the fruit along the Silk Route to Persia. Spaniards brought peaches to the Americas. The Natchez people, of what is now the southeastern United States, became so enamored of the fruit that they named one of their months after it.

Peacock *(1598)*   114

From Latin *pavo*, "peafowl," combined with Middle English *cok*, "male bird, rooster" from Latin *coco*, an onomatopoetic word for the bird's cackling. Male peacocks show brilliant-colored feathers during their courtship displays; the female peahen has a more somber color that provides camouflage while she is nesting. The pigment in peacock feathers is actually brown or black melanin (see page 125), but the brilliant color comes from what scientists call interference. The melanin particles create a film through which the light must pass. Light is reflected by both the top and bottom surfaces of the film. The light that travels to the bottom and back is slowed down, and when it rejoins the light reflected from the top surface, the waves are no longer identical. The two waves "interfere" with each other: some colors in the spectrum get canceled out, while others are intensified. The resulting color depends on how far the light must travel to reach the lower surface and return.

Pearl White *(1590)*   184

Various mollusks, including mussels, clams, and oysters, make pearls by secreting layers of calcium carbonate around an irritant, like a grain of sand. The name may come from late Latin *perula*, "little pear"; or from *sphaerula*, "little sphere," or even from Latin *pernula*, "little ham," because of the shape of the mussel's stalk-like foot. A pearl is like the mollusk's shell in reverse, with the iridescent layer on the outside. The pearl's sheen, or luster, comes from the way each of the layers bends and reflects light slightly differently. The color of a pearl depends on the depth of the water in which the mollusk lives; what's in the water, including pollutants; and whether the pearl forms near the liver or the intestine. Until the seventeenth century, people thought that pearls began as dewdrops. The oyster was thought to rise to the surface of the water periodically, open its shell, and take in a drop of dew. According to this theory, the weather at the time the oyster surfaced would affect the color of the pearl. If it was raining, the pearl would be pale; if it was misting, the pearl would look muddy; and if it thundered, the oyster would snap its shell shut, and there would be no pearl at all. But if the day was clear, the pearl would be white.

Periwinkle *(1902)*   149
The color of the flower, from Latin *per*, "through," and *vincire*, "to bind," describing the behavior of the vine.

Petunia *(1891)*   176
The color of the flower. In the Guaraní language of southern Brazil, *petÿ* is the name of the tobacco plant, to which the petunia is related.

Pewter *(1924)*   187
The color of the metal, an alloy of tin with lead, copper, or other metals. From Old French *peautre*, possibly a corruption of *spelter*, "zinc."

Phlox Purple *(1886)* 164
The color of the flower, from the Greek *phlóx*, "flame."

Phthalocyanine Blue *(1935)* 140
A painter's color invented in the twentieth century. "Phthalo" comes from "naphtha," an oil produced by distilling petroleum or coal, whose name ultimately comes from the Avestan *napta*, "moist." The second part of the name comes from "cyan" (see page 39). The coloring material in phthalocyanine is closely related to the hemin pigments that make blood red and the chlorophyll that makes leaves green.

Pigeon's Throat *(1839)* 129
Pigeon comes from Latin *pipire*, "to chirp"; throat comes from an Indo-European root that means "to swell." The iridescent colors of a pigeon's throat come from interference (see Peacock, page 108).

Pine Green *(1942)* (Pine Needle *(1927)*) 133
The color of pine needles. From the Latin *pinus*, "pine tree," which is related to Sanskrit *pítuh*, "sap, juice, resin, food." One pine tree in California is believed to be over 4,700 years old.

Pink *(1681)* 13
The color of the flower. Probably from Dutch *pinken*, "to blink," which came to mean "small"; the flower's name was probably originally "pink eye," or "small eye," as it is in French: *oeillet*. But another possible origin is the verb "to pink," which meant to prick or cut at the edges, as with pinking shears. The jagged petals of the flower looked as though they had been cut, and so, perhaps, it became the "pink."

Pistachio Green *(1789)* 93
The color of the nut, from its Persian name, *pistah*.

Pitch Black *(1599)* 191
Old English *pic*, from Latin *pix*, "pitch," or pine tar, is related to Greek words for turpentine and fir tree. All of these come from a root that means "to be fat," referring to the tree's oozing resin. In the sixteenth and seventeenth centuries, European shipbuilders covered the hulls of ships with pitch to protect them from mollusks that would otherwise destroy the wood and sink the ships.

Platinum *(1918)* 186
The color of the precious metal, from Spanish *platina*, a diminutive of *plata*, "silver," ultimately from Old Provençal *plata* or Old French *plate*, "a sheet of metal."

Plum *(1805)* 175
Anglo-Saxon *plūme*, comes from Latin *prunus*, and Greek *prounon*, "plum tree," and thus the same root as Prune (1789), also used as a color name.

Pompadour Rose *(1756)* 23
The color takes its name from the Marquise de Pompadour, the mistress of Louis XV of France; the marquise took an interest in the manufacture of porcelain, and designed many pieces in this color. One company of British troops became known as the Pompadours because they used the color in their regimental dress.

Pompeiian Red *(1882)* 25
The color takes its name from the southern Italian city buried by lava in the eruption of Mount Vesuvius in the

year 79 C.E.; the color was found on the walls of many houses when Pompeii was first excavated in 1748.

Pontiff Purple *(1900)*   172
The color of the robes of a pope or bishop, from Latin *pontifex*, "high priest," probably from Latin *facere*, "to make," and an Osco-Umbrian root *puntis*, a propitiatory offering: the priest was the person who made offerings to the gods.

Poppy *(1705)*   27
The color of the flower, from Latin *papaver*, "poppy," which may come from a root that means "to swell, to blow." The scentless flowers are pollinated by a species of beetle that is attracted by anything red—even a red beach pail.

Primrose Yellow *(1629)*   3
The color of the flower. From Latin *primula veris*, "firstling of spring." In Old English this became *primole*, which by association with the familiar flower "rose" formed "primrose." Primroses ordinarily have five petals; a six-petaled primrose is said to bring luck.

Prussian Blue *(1724)*   137
See page 100.

Puce *(1787)*   34
The French word for "flea." Marie Antoinette created such a rage for clothes in puce that dressmakers kept coming up with new shades, including *tête de puce*, *cuisse de puce*, and *ventre de puce*, or "flea's head," "flea's thigh," and flea's belly."

Pumpkin *(1922)*   52

The color of the fruit. From Greek *pepon*, "cooked" or "ripe" (see page 11). Pumpkins can be amazingly prolific: one seventeenth-century Massachusetts man dropped a pumpkin in his field and found 260 pumpkins there the next year.

Purple *(975)*   170

See page 118.

Putty *(1889)*   69

The original putty was jeweler's polish made by roasting tin in a pot; its name probably comes from French *potée*, "potful." Some people say that putty was actually made from ground-up old tin pots, which gave it its name; in either case, "pot" comes from Latin *potare*, "to drink."

is for Quail,
Quartz Green, Quercitron,
Quince Yellow, and
Quaker Gray

Quaker Gray *(1880)*
(Quaker Color *(1770)*) 107

"Quaker" is the nickname outsiders gave to the Society of Friends, a religious sect whose founder, George Fox, preached that worshipers should "quake and tremble at the word of the Lord." Friends were pacifists, opposed to all war and killing, and to slavery and capital punishment. They were early advocates of women's rights. They also spurned painting, music, and theater, and maintained simplicity in both speech and dress. Although Friends were never required or forbidden to wear specific colors, they were expected to dress unobtrusively. In 1693, one of the most famous Quakers, William Penn, who founded the colony of Pennsylvania, wrote that "the more simple and plain" Quakers' clothes were, "the better. Neither unshapely, nor fantastical, and for Use and Decency, not for Pride." Accordingly, Quakers tended to choose clothes in drabs, grays, and browns, which became known as Quaker colors. (At one point, however, an Englishman named

Brown wrote a pamphlet ridiculing the Friends, and for a time, Friends refused to wear brown clothing.)

The Society of Friends founded schools that emphasized science, and the sect has produced many notable scientists. Among them was John Dalton, one of the founders of modern chemistry. At twelve, Dalton was already teaching school, even though some of his students were sixteen- and seventeen-year-olds who threatened to beat up their teacher in the local graveyard.

Dalton was one of the first scientists to describe red-green color blindness, from which he himself suffered. He described the strange confusions of his vision: blushing cheeks looked "dusky blue" to him; blood looked bottle green; bright red sealing wax was identical in color to a laurel leaf or grass; the fruit and the leaves of a cherry tree were one and the same color. This condition was later called "Daltonism" in his honor. Curiously, Dalton was also one of the first scientists to write about the causes of the aurora borealis, or Northern Lights, which are known for the beauty of their colors.

Dalton always dressed soberly, in the tradition of the Quakers. The story was told that he once bought a pair of silk stockings as a birthday present for his mother to give her a change from her hand-knit drab woolen hose. Dalton's mother thanked him for the "grand pair of hose," but wondered aloud what had made him "fancy such a bright color." She certainly could not attend Friends' meetings in such stockings! Dalton, to whom the stockings seemed a perfectly sober gray, showed them to his brother, who took his side: of course they were a "proper go-to-meeting" color.

The two Dalton brothers shared the trait of color blindness, and even though they disagreed with their mother about the color of the silk stockings, they had actually inherited their color blindness from her. Hereditary traits, like the brothers' red-green color blindness, pass from one generation to the next in the form of information carried in parts of our cells called chromosomes. Human beings have 23 pairs of chromosomes. One of those pairs is different in men and women: in women, the pair is made up of two X chromosomes, one from each parent; in men, the pair has one X chromosome, inherited from the mother, and one Y chromosome, inherited from the father. The gene for Daltonism occurs only on the X chromosome, and is recessive, which means that it will always remain hidden in the presence of the dominant gene for normal color vision. If a woman, who has two X chromosomes, inherits the gene for Daltonism on only one of her X chromosomes, from either parent, she will still have normal color vision, as long as her other X chromosome carries the dominant gene. She will be red-green color blind only if she inherits the gene on both X chromosomes, one from her father and one from her mother. But even if she has normal color vision, she can still pass the gene for Daltonism on to her children.

The Y chromosome contains no information about red-green color blindness. It has no place for the dominant gene for normal color vision. So a man's red-green color vision depends entirely on the X chromosome he inherits from his mother. The sons of a woman with normal vision who carries the gene for Daltonism on one X chromosome have a 50-50 chance of inheriting the gene for Daltonism, depending on which of their mother's X chromosomes they receive. If they inherit the X chromosome with the gene for Daltonism, as both Dalton brothers did, they will be red-green color-blind, even though their mother's color vision is normal.

When the Dalton brothers looked at the silk stockings, both saw the same gray color. They agreed that their mother must have something wrong with *her* eyes. Outnumbered, Dalton's mother took the stockings, which looked "red as a cherry" to her, and showed them to her neighbors, who all agreed with her that they were "varra fine stuff, but uncommon scarlety!"

Quail *(1920)* 70
The color of the bird, from medieval Latin *quaccola*, which sounds like the bird's call. One variety is known as a "fool quail" because it doesn't like to fly, even when it is in danger.

Quartz Green *(1934)* 117
One shade of the mineral whose name comes from German *quarz*, of Slavic origin, probably related to Old Slavic *tvrŭdŭ* and Lithuanian *tvirtas*, "hard." The Inuit of Alaska once believed that quartz was ice so completely frozen it had become stone.

Quercitron *(1775)* 38
A pigment made from the inner bark of the *Quercus tinctoria* tree, whose name in Latin means "dyer's oak."

Quince Yellow *(1398)* 63
The color of the fruit, from Greek *kodumalon*, which is usually thought to mean "apple of Cydonia," a city in Crete, but may come from an even older name from Asia Minor. The Portuguese word for quince is *marmelo*, from which we get "marmelade." The ancient inhabitants of Baghdad used the aromatic quince to perfume their tents, and Romans used it to perfume their reception rooms.

*is for Raspberry,
Robin's Egg Blue, Rose,
Ruby, and Royal Purple*

Royal Purple *(1661)* 177

"Royal" comes from the Latin *regalis*, meaning "belonging to a monarch." When you hear "royal," you may think of blue, but the royal color of the ancients was, without question, purple. In the ancient world, however, purple didn't mean exactly what it means today. It simply meant any shade of dye that could be extracted from certain types of shellfish, notably the murex and the buccinum. The Greeks called all dye-producing varieties of shellfish *porphyry*, which became *purpura* in Latin, and purple in English.

The root of *porphyry* means "to mix," "to knead," or "to stir violently." Homer uses *porphyry* to describe the turbulent, restless motion of waves. The dye probably got its name from both the stirring motions of the dyer and the rapidly changing color of the dye. The *porphyry* shellfish's glands contained a milky white fluid. On exposure to light and air, the fluid turned from white to cream to yellow to green. After several dippings, the cloth would reach its final color, which ranged from scarlet to violet to brown to black, depending on the species of mollusk, the season, the weather, the age of the mollusks, and even what they had eaten. One prized shade of purple was called *blatta*, the Latin name for certain insects such as the cockroach and the flea. The Roman naturalist Pliny declared that the most valued shade of purple was "the color of congealed blood."

Entire cities in the ancient world made their fortunes from purple dyeing; of these, Tyre was the most famous. The Tyrians claimed that a god named Melkarth had discovered the dye on their own shores. One day Melkarth was out walking by the sea when his dog bit open a shellfish, which instantly stained its mouth purple. Inspired, Melkarth gathered more shells and used them to dye a gown for his beloved, a nymph named Tyros.

In tribute to the source of the city's prosperity, the coins of Tyre showed a dog sniffing at a murex shell. Well might the dog sniff—no one much liked the smell of purple. Preparing the dye involved allowing the shellfish to decompose; on exposure to light, the dye started to smell like garlic. As early as 2,000 B.C.E., a papyrus described the sad life of the dyer: "His hands stink, they have the odor of rotten fish, and he abhors the sight of all cloth." Surprisingly, given its unappealing odor, both Roman men and women used purple to color their cheeks and lips.

In 1864, at Sidon in what is now Lebanon, archaeologists discovered a mound of seashells almost 400 feet long and 25 feet high. It took some 20,000 shellfish to dye one square yard of fabric, so only the very rich could afford purple cloth. In the fourth century, one pound of wool dyed with Tyrian purple cost as much as a baker earned for one thousand days' work; a teacher of Greek or Latin literature would have to tutor a pupil for twenty-five months to afford that pound of wool. To wear purple, therefore, was a sign of high birth or status. Alexander the Great wore purple, sat beneath purple canopies, and walked on purple carpets. Cleopatra's flagship had purple sails. The Roman emperor Caligula covered his favorite horse with purple; in order to display his wealth, the emperor Nero had the wild animals that appeared in the arena dyed purple. After the seat of the Roman empire moved to Byzantium, the empresses gave birth in a chamber lined with purple; their children were called *porphyrogenitos*, or "born to the purple."

When a ruler gave someone a purple garment, it was a clear sign of favor. In the Bible, Belshazzar honors Daniel with a purple robe for deciphering the writing on the wall; in the Book of Esther, the Persian king Ahasuerus dresses Mordecai in purple to thank him for saving his life.

But emperors didn't want just anyone to walk around in the royal color, looking like a member of the royal family or one of their close friends. When Nero saw a woman at one of his recitals dressed in purple, he had her stripped first of all her clothes and then of all her possessions. In the year 424, the Byzantine emperor Theodosius, who wore a purple diadem, purple robe, purple trousers, and purple shoes, pronounced that anyone caught wearing the royal shades of purple would be guilty of treason and put to death. Not surprisingly, this edict caused a noticeable decline in the purple industry.

Raspberry *(1892)*   14
The color of the fruit, from Old High German *hrespan*,

"to rake," referring to the plant's thorns. The early German name, *Kratsberre*, translates as "scratchberry."

Raven Black *(1600)*   191
The color of the glossy feathers of the bird, whose name comes from Old English *hraefn*, an onomatopoetic word imitating the bird's croaking call, and related to Latin *crepare*, "to croak, to chatter."

Raw Sienna *(1700s)*   43
See page 128.

Raw Umber *(1658)*   74
See page 140.

Red *(700)*   56
See page 98.

Reseda Green *(1873)*   128
From the Latin *resedare*, "to allay, to assuage, to heal," because the plant was supposed to reduce tumors. One variety of reseda produced one of the oldest-known yellow dyes: weld.

Roan *(1530)*   78
Roan is a color of horses: a roan horse has a bay or chestnut coat mixed with gray or white; the name may come from a Germanic word for red or from the Latin *ravus*, "gray, grayish yellow, tawny."

Robin's Egg Blue *(1873)*   119
The bird's name is a diminutive of Robert, which comes from Old High German *hrodeberht*, "glory-bright." The coloration of birds' eggs often acts as camouflage to

hide the egg from predators, particularly when the bird lays its eggs near the ground; the robin lays her eggs under greenery. The color of the robin's egg comes from a pigment in bile, a secretion of the liver, that is deposited on the egg just before it is laid.

Rose *(1382)* 12

The color of the flower, from its Latin name, *rosa*, from an Indo-European root that means "thorn, bramble." The rose is an extremely ancient flower: rose fossils have been found dating back 32 million years. In Roman legend, Cupid bribed the god of silence with a rose so that he would not say a word about Venus's romantic adventures. The rose became a symbol of secrecy. Roman hosts would hang roses over the dining table to remind their guests not to tell others whatever secrets they learned over dinner. In later centuries, hosts would have a large rose painted or carved above their dining tables. Thus a conversation held in confidence became known as *sub rosa*: "beneath the rose." The Roman emperor Heliogabalus, who was famous for excess—he liked to bathe in a swimming pool filled with rose water—also liked roses overhead at dinner: at the end of the meal, he would have his guests showered with roses from openings in the ceiling. He did tend to overdo it, however, and occasionally drowned his guests in roses, which was one way to insure that they wouldn't repeat his secrets.

Royal Blue *(1789)* 141

(For the etymology of "royal," see page 118.)

The association of blue with royalty has several possible sources. Some people suggest that France's Louis XIV, the Sun King, had his robes, and the robes of his men, dyed with indigo (see page 68). Others link the color to the British Order of the Garter, founded by King Edward III in 1348. Legend has it that the king was dancing with Joan of Kent, the Countess of Salisbury, when one of her blue garters fell to the floor. The king retrieved it and put it on himself, declaring *"Honi soit qui mal y pense,"* or "Shame to him who thinks evil," which became the order's motto. The Order of the Garter is the most prestigious honor in England, and recipients still receive a blue garter.

Ruby *(1572)* 29
The color of the precious stone, from Latin *rubeus*, "red" (see page 98). Medieval and Renaissance scholars thought that the ruby's color meant that it was ripe, and that the color deepened with time. "If the ruby is taken too soon from its cradle, the mine," said one seventeenth-century writer, "before it is seasoned by the sun, it remains pale." In Burmese legend, a ruby would make its owner invulnerable, but not if worn as jewelry: it had to be embedded in the owner's flesh.

Russet *(1562)* 77
From Old French *rousset*, ultimately from *roux*, "red" (see page 98). Originally, russet referred to a reddish homespun cloth; eventually the cloth gave its name to the color.

Rust *(1692)* 58
A Germanic word going back to an Indo-European root that means "red" (see page 98).

 **is for Sable,
Saffron, Silver,
Strawberry,
and Sepia**

Sepia *(1821)*

Sēpia is the Greek name for the cuttlefish, a relative of the octopus and squid. All three belong to a class of mollusks called Cephalopoda, from Greek roots meaning "head" and "foot." One look will tell you why: their bodies are almost entirely head and feet, with not much in between. *Sēpia* comes from the Greek root *sēpein*, which means "to make rotten, to befoul, to make filthy," which is exactly what the cuttlefish does to seawater when it squirts its ink. (The same root explains why we use an "antiseptic" on a wound.) One cuttlefish can cloud thousands of gallons of water in seconds, which is a pretty effective way to hide from predators, especially because it takes the cuttlefish only fifteen minutes to replenish its supply of ink.

The ink sac, or chromatophore, performs another important function for the cuttlefish. As the ink sac changes shape, the cuttlefish's color changes. When the chromatophore is tiny, like a balloon before you blow it up, all the pigment is concentrated in a small space; on a signal from the cuttlefish's brain, the ink sac expands into a thin disk, so that the pigment spreads over a large area. Just as humans blush when embarrassed, a cuttlefish will change color when it is alarmed or under attack, when it goes on the offensive, and when it rests. (The Murray Islanders, who call the cuttlefish *gole*, have a color called *golegole*. At first, English speakers assumed *golegole* was the same color as sepia, but instead, it seems to mean something multicolored or changeable, like the cuttlefish itself.)

The ink of the cuttlefish, and the ink's color, also became known as sepia. The Romans knew that you could write with the sepia's ink, which became popular for drawing and watercolors in the eighteenth century, and formed part of the emulsion, or coating, of photographic paper in the nineteenth.

Sepia lasts longer than any other natural ink. In the early nineteenth century, a paleontologist discovered a fossil relative of the sepia with its ink sac intact. He dipped his pen in the 150-million-year-old ink and used it to draw the illustration that accompanied the description of his discovery.

The pigment in the sepia's ink is melanin, from the Greek root *melan*, meaning "black" or "ink." Melanin is also responsible for all the colors of human skin except that of albinos, whose skin contains no pigment; and for all the brown, black, red, and gold colors of mammalian hair and fur. The only exception is the red hair of humans, which is colored by a pigment that contains iron. All human eye color comes from melanin, too, except for blue eyes, which actually contain no pigment at all. Their color comes from the scattering of high-energy blue light by tiny white particles in the eye, the same phenomenon that makes the sky blue.

Sable *(1374)* 110

The fur of the mammal; from Old Russian *sobol*, ultimately from an East Asiatic language.

Saffron *(1200)* 39

The color of the spice, made from the dried stigmas of the flower *Crocus sativus*. The name comes from Arabic *za'farān*, related to *asfar*, "a yellow plant, yellow." As a dye, saffron is extremely potent: one part of saffron will color one hundred thousand parts of water. The robes of Buddhist monks are traditionally dyed with saffron. It takes about four thousand stigmas to produce one ounce of dye, which consequently has often been worth more than its weight in gold. (The ceiling of the Saffron Guild's building in Basel, Switzerland, is painted with both gold and powdered saffron.) In fifteenth-century Nuremburg, you could be put to death for counterfeiting the dye. One man convicted of this crime was burned at the stake over a fire made from his own imitation saffron.

Sage Green *(1596)* 99

The color of the herb, from Latin *salvus*, "healthy, saved," because of the herb's medicinal qualities. It was the foremost medicinal herb of the Middle Ages, considered a cure for epilepsy, lethargy, palsy, cramp, and plague.

Salmon *(1776)* 21

The color of the fish, from French *saumon*, and ultimately from Latin *salire*, "to leap"—salmon is "the leaping fish."

Sand *(1627)* 68

The name comes from Middle English *sond*, which is related to Greek words for "small stone, pebble" and "to crumble away."

Sap Green *(1578)* 94
An artist's pigment originally made from the unripe berries of the buckthorn plant. "Sap" comes from Old English *saep*, probably from Latin *sapa*, "boiled juice."

Sapphire *(1430)* 150
The color of the gemstone. From Hebrew *sappīr*, "sapphire, lapis lazuli," and possibly from Sanskrit *śani-priya*, "dear to the planet Saturn."

Scarlet *(1250)* 26
See page 141.

Seafoam Green *(1892)* 124
From Old English *sǣ*, "sea, lake," and *fām*, "foam, froth." The sea's color is in part a reflection of the sky, but seawater itself is slightly colored and absorbs red light, reflecting back a light that is greener than the sky.

Seal Brown *(1881)* 83
The color of the animal, from its Old English name *seolh*.

Shell Pink *(1865)* 8
Anglo-Saxon *sciell*, which meant "peel, rind, husk, eggshell," came from a Germanic root that means "to separate": a shell is a covering that separates, or peels off.

Shocking Pink *(1936)* 16
From French *choquer*, possibly meaning "to bump up against," and related to Old French *choque*, "tree stump." The color was invented by the designer Elsa

Schiaparelli, and was shocking because it was so unlike the delicate pinks the fashion world was used to.

Shrimp Pink *(1895)* 20
From Middle English *shrimpe*, probably related to the Middle German *schrimpfen*, "to shrink up."

Sienna *(1760)* 59
An artist's pigment, made from the earth near Siena, in Italy. Used either raw or burnt.

Silver *(1481)* 186
The color of the precious metal. From Old English *siolfor*, "silver," ultimately from Akkadian *ṣarāpu*, "to smelt, to refine," Assyrian *ṣurrupu*, "purify, smelt," and *ṣarpu*, "silver."

Sky Blue *(1728)* 144
From Old Norse *skȳ*, "cloud," and ultimately from Sanskrit *ska*, "to hide, to cover." The color of the sky is due to tiny particles that scatter the high-energy blue wavelengths of light, a phenomenon called "Tyndall scattering" after the scientist who discovered it.

Slate Blue *(1796)* 143
The color of the stone, which splits easily, from French *esclat*, "splinter, fragment."

Smoke Gray *(1805)* 188
From Old English *smēocan*, "to give off smoke," which is related to Greek *smugenai*, "be consumed with heat." The tiny particles in smoke reflect blue light; against a light background, smoke appears blue, but it looks brown or gray when the background is dark.

Snow White *(1000)*   182
From Anglo-Saxon *snāw*, "snow," related to Sanskrit *snēhaš*, "stickiness."

Sorrel *(1469)*   47
A color of horses, whose name comes from Old French *sorel*. Sorrel is related to Germanic words that meant "dry" and were used to refer to the color of autumn leaves.

Spice Brown *(1922)*   72
From Latin *species*, "kind, sort," which in Late Latin came to mean "wares, articles of merchandise." Spices were among the most important items of trade in the Renaissance, and the cause of many of the most famous European voyages of exploration.

Spinach Green *(1896)*   131
From the Persian name of the vegetable, *aspanākh*, which some etymologists translate "green hand." Well into the nineteenth century, cooks used the bright green water in which spinach had been cooked as a food coloring for cakes and desserts.

Spring Green *(1766)*   91
The color of the first leaves of the season, when plants spring from the earth. The season takes its name from the Old English verb *springan*, "to spring," related to the Greek word for "to hasten," and the Sanskrit for "to desire."

Spruce Green *(1916)*   128
The color of the tree, from Middle English *Pruce*, meaning "Prussia," where it was widely grown. When

spruce trees are injured, they exude a resin, known as "spruce gum," to seal the wound. Bears like to swallow large chunks of spruce gum before they go into hibernation, and in many parts of Europe, people enjoyed spruce gum as we enjoy chewing gum today.

Steel Blue *(1817)*   143
The color of the metal, from Old English *style*, which comes from a Teutonic root meaning "to be firm, to be rigid, to resist."

Straw *(1589)*   63
From Old English *strēowian*, "to strew," since straw is strewn in stables.

Strawberry *(1675)*   25
The color of the fruit, the origin of whose name is obscure: perhaps the seeds resembled bits of straw, or the plant put out strawlike runners; or perhaps they are "strayberries," from the way the new growth wanders.

Sulphur Yellow *(1805)*   102
The color of the element, from its Latin name, *sulfur*, probably related to *sälp*, which means "to burn" in Tocharian, an ancient member of the Indo-European family of languages, spoken in Chinese Turkestan until a thousand years ago.

Sunflower Yellow *(1892)*   37
The Old English word *sunne* comes from an ancient Indo-European root that means "to shine." Flower comes from the Latin *flores*, "flower," from an Indo-European root that means "to bloom." Sunflowers, which turn to follow the sun's course during the day, can grow to be 12 feet tall.

is for Tangerine,
Tattletale Gray,
Topaz, and Turquoise

Turquoise *(1573)* 118

Turquoise is a shortened version of the French *pierre turquoise*, or "Turkish stone." Turquoise actually came from Persia and the Sinai peninsula, but it reached Europe via Turkey, and the association stuck. (The turkey got its name the same way. The American bird reminded Europeans of a bird that did not come from Turkey, but had come through Turkey on its way to Europe.)

Turquoise generally occurs in dry places, like deserts, where occasional rainfall washes elements out of the rocks; when the water evaporates, the mixture of elements that's left forms turquoise. This doesn't happen overnight: the turquoise miners of Persia used to say that while a cherry ripens in a season, the sun takes a thousand years to ripen a turquoise. The color of turquoise comes from its copper content, which is why weathered copper statues or oxidized pennies may remind you of turquoise.

As a color, turquoise occupies a curious place on the border between blue and green. Many languages do not

131

distinguish between blue and green at all, using the same word for both. The Highland Scots, for example, call both sky and grass "gorm." Ancient Chinese had a single word for blue and green; in order to translate "blue" and "green" from other languages, modern Chinese uses the word for sapphire to mean "blue" and the word for emerald to mean "green." Many Native American languages of both North and South America have a single word for both blue and green. One anthropologist reports that the Western Apache use the same word, *dukliž*, for a range of colors "from light blue to rich Kelly green, the color of all grasses, all bush and tree leaves, the eyes of an Appaloosa horse (perhaps the lightest blue there is) and the color of underwater algae, perhaps the darkest green."

As it happens, *dukliž* is also the Western Apache word for turquoise. The American Southwest is rich in turquoise, which Native American peoples have mined for centuries. To some Western Apaches, the stone had magical properties: if you attached a tiny piece of turquoise to a bow or gun, the weapon would shoot straight. According to a Western Apache saying, after a storm, if you follow a rainbow to its end and search the ground, you will find not a pot of gold, but turquoise buried in the damp earth.

The Zuñi, another of the peoples of the Southwest, say that turquoise represents both the blue of heaven and the green of earth and that the color of the sky is actually a reflection of the Mountain of Turquoise. The Zuñi traditionally placed a small turquoise in their cradleboards, just beneath where the child's heart would lie, to give the cradleboard "a good heart" and make sure it protected the child.

Like the Western Apache, the Navajo use a single

word, *dott'ish*, for the turquoise stone and for the colors green and blue. The Navajo, or, as they call themselves in their own language, the Dineh—the People—say that the heart of the earth is made of turquoise. In the Origin Legend of the Dineh, First Man made the sun out of a turquoise disk and gave it to Sun Bearer to carry across the sky. When the sky was blue and free of clouds, the Dineh would say that the Sun Bearer had mounted his turquoise steed. But when the wind blew furiously, the Dineh would say that the wind spirit was searching for turquoises. Until he found them, he would not allow the clouds to form and make rain.

One of the most revered deities among the Dineh is Turquoise Woman. According to the Origin Legend, one day First Man heard the sound of a child crying, and followed the cries to a mountain whose peak was hidden by clouds and lightning. A giant rainbow touched the earth, dyeing the mountain with its intense colors. First Man climbed to the top of the mountain and discovered a small turquoise figure rocking in a cradle of rainbows made of Dawn and Turquoise. He brought her home, and he and First Woman nursed her as if she were their own child. The figure came to life and became Turquoise Woman, who is also known as Changing Woman, because she changes with the seasons. When the Dineh were wandering through the earth and nearly dying of thirst, Changing Woman gave them a rod of turquoise; wherever they struck the earth with the rod, water sprang up to sustain them.

The Origin Legend tells of the ascent of the Dineh to the world we live in through four other worlds, which rest inside one another like inverted bowls. In one version of the Origin Legend, the Ant People were the first to emerge into this upper world, bringing soil and seeds with them. To create a tunnel to this world, they bit off chunks of the fourth world's hard sky and carried them to the surface of this one. Wherever they deposited those chunks of sky, you will find turquoise today.

Tan *(1590)* 44
In Celtic, *tann* is an oak tree; since oak and other barks were used to cure, or "tan," leather, the tree gave its name to the color of treated leather.

Tangerine *(1899)* 53
The color of the fruit, which takes its name from Tangier in Morocco, the port from which the fruit was first shipped to Europe, in 1841.

Tattletale Gray *(1943)* 185
"Tattletale" is onomatopoetic, from Middle Flemish *tatelen*, "gabble, cackle." The color was a "tattletale" because it gave away the secret that something hadn't been laundered properly. The idea of tattling was particularly powerful during World War II, when the color was named, because, as the wartime slogan warned, "Loose Lips Sink Ships."

Taupe *(1911)* 184
From the French *taupe*, "mole."

Tawny *(1377)* 45
In French "tan" (see above) became *tenné*, which came back into English as tawny.

Teal *(1941)* 116
The color of the sea bird, *tele* in Middle English, possibly related to a Dutch word that means "to breed."

Terra Cotta *(1882)*   46
The color of a type of pottery made from fine clay and sand, whose name comes from Italian, meaning "baked earth." "Terra" ultimately comes from a root that means "to be dry": the earth is the dry place.

Thistle *(1892)*   169
The color of the flower, from its Old English name *thistel*, which comes from an Indo-European root that means "to prick, stick, pierce," probably related to Sanskrit *tiktáḥ*, "sharp," and a Greek word meaning "to prick." Legend has it that in the tenth century a troop of Danish invaders was trying to sneak up on the Scottish army and took off their shoes to walk across a moat. One of them stepped on a thistle and cried out so loudly that the Scottish soldiers woke up, armed themselves, and chased off the Danes. Thus the thistle became the national emblem of Scotland.

Titanium White *(1920)*   182
An artist's pigment, first manufactured in 1916 from titanium oxide. The element titanium gets its name from the Greek Titans, the mythical giant offspring of Uranus, god of Heaven, and Gaea, goddess of the Earth.

Titian *(1896)*   44
The reddish color of hair favored by the sixteenth-century painter Titian (Tiziano Vecellio).

Toast *(1922)*   47
From Latin *torrere*, "to parch, burn, roast."

Tobacco *(1789)*   76
In the Arawak or Taino language of Haiti, *tabaco* re-

ferred either to the Y-shaped pipe or the cigar-shaped roll in which the leaf was smoked. In Europe it may have combined with an earlier Arabic word, *ṭabbâq*, meaning "medicinal herbs." Europeans learned about tobacco from the inhabitants of the Americas and almost immediately began to argue about whether it was good or bad for a body. A sixteenth-century visitor to Guatemala and Nicaragua called tobacco "a pestiferous and wicked poison from the devil." In 1616 one Englishman wrote a will leaving all his household goods to his son on the condition that if any of his other children found the son using tobacco, that son or daughter would immediately inherit everything. The story is told that Sir Walter Raleigh once asked a servant to bring him some ale, and then lit a pipe. The servant, who had never seen tobacco, returned with the ale and saw the smoke around Raleigh's face. He assumed Raleigh was on fire and promptly doused him with the ale.

Tomato *(1891)* 57

When explorers first brought tomatoes back to Europe from South America, many people feared they were poisonous, perhaps noting their resemblance to their cousin, deadly nightshade. One German botanist advised the fruit "should not be taken internally." The Pilgrims of Massachusetts, suspicious of the fruit, actually fired a minister for growing them in his garden. Nevertheless, North American colonists, including George Washington, continued to grow tomatoes—but only for decoration. Americans did not change their minds about tomatoes until the early nineteenth century, when Colonel Robert Gibbon Johnson of Salem, New Jersey, announced that he would eat an entire basket of the "wolf peaches" (a literal translation of their Latin name,

Lycopersicon) on the courthouse steps, just to prove that they were not poisonous. Crowds gathered to see Johnson meet his doom—but he survived, and convinced the nation that tomatoes were, in Johnson's words, "a delight to the eye, a joy to the palate."

Topaz *(1572)* 42

The color of the gemstone. Possibly from Greek *topazein*, "to conjecture," because the Greeks believed that the stone came from an island hidden by clouds and fog whose location they could only guess. More likely the name comes from Sanskrit *tapas*, "heat, fire," from *tap*, "to shine."

U is for Umber and Ultramarine

Ultramarine *(1598)* 153

In the fifteenth century, England began to trade with Venice. By the sixteenth century, Italy had become the fashionable place for English travelers to visit. Those who appreciated art would certainly have heard the Italians discussing *azzurro oltromarino*, perhaps the most famous, and certainly the most expensive pigment in Italy. These travelers tended to bring Italian words back with them as souvenirs; in English, the Venetian pigment became "ultramarine blue," and eventually simply "ultramarine."

"Ultramarine" comes from Latin words that mean "beyond" and "sea." While that might lead you to think the name means deep-sea blue or bluer-than-the-sea blue, what it really means is "the blue brought from across the sea": overseas or imported blue. (*Azurro citramarino* meant blue from this side of the sea.) Ultramarine was made from lapis lazuli, a semiprecious stone imported to Venice from Badakhshan in what is now Afghanistan. Real lapis lazuli—for there were many imitations—contains flecks of pyrite, or fools' gold, like stars glittering in the night sky. *Lapis* is the Latin word for "stone," and *lazuli* comes from the Persian word for "blue," *lazhward*, which gave Italian *azzurro* and gave English "azure" (see page 18).

In the east, blue pigment from lapis lazuli graced Byzantine manuscripts and Persian miniatures. In Italy, painters ground and soaked the lapis lazuli, extracting its color in stages. The first extraction of ultramarine was worth twice its weight in gold. By the end of the process, almost no blue was left in the stone. This final color was called "ultramarine ash."

In 1437, Cennino Cennini, author of *The Book of the Artist*, wrote, "Ultramarine blue is the most perfect, noble, and beautiful color, above all the others, about which one can neither do nor say anything to add to its perfection." The Virgin Mary's robes were almost always painted in the finest grade of ultramarine as a sign of reverence. In the fifteenth century, patrons' contracts with painters often specified the cost of the ultramarine blue the painter would use. Ghirlandaio's contract for the Adoration of the Magi specified that he would use ultramarine costing four florins per ounce—more than his monthly salary. In 1824 a French society for the advancement of industry offered a prize of 6,000 francs to anyone would could figure out how to make artificial ultramarine for less than 300 francs per kilogram.

The dukes and princes who commissioned paintings often paid separately for the ultramarine, and bought only enough for the work at hand. Since painters couldn't afford to buy ultramarine for themselves, they would wash their brushes painstakingly, hoping to retrieve a tiny bit of pigment they could save for themselves. According to the biographer Vasari, when the painter Perugino had a commission from the convent of the Ingesuati, the convent's prior mixed the ultramarine blue himself. Whenever Perugino needed to use it, the prior would be right there watching him. Perugino resorted to the old trick of washing his brushes. When the painting was finished, he handed all the pigment he had managed to steal back to the prior, telling him he should be more trusting in the future.

Umber *(1600)* 80
An artist's pigment, made from earth gathered in the Italian province of Umbria. Used either raw or burnt.

V is for Vandyke Brown, Venetian Red, Verdigris, Violet, and Vermilion

Vermilion (1400)   56

Vermilion was the brightest red pigment known to the ancient world. Its name, which comes from the Latin *vermiculus*, or "little worm," refers to the insects that produce the dyes called kermes and cochineal. To make these dyes, you had to scrape the female insects off the plants they lived on (according to one account, women with long fingernails used to do this job), kill them with heat, and then grind them into a powder.

Kermes is the oldest known red dye in the world. In one neolithic grotto in France, archaeologists have found both fibers and food dyed with kermes, the food perhaps for magical or medicinal reasons. "Kermes" comes from the Arabic *qirmiz*, meaning "worm," which also gives us the color names "crimson" and "carmine." "Scarlet," too, owes its name to the insect: in Persian, *säqirlät* meant cloth dyed with kermes. The Romans used kermes to dye generals' cloaks. They valued the dye so highly that Roman armies accepted kermes as part of their tribute from conquered nations. In the Middle Ages, landlords took kermes in payment of rent. Kermes gave the characteristic red color both to the Islamic fez and to the skullcaps of Catholic cardinals.

Cochineal, closely related to kermes but a stronger dye, was known to the Aztecs in Mexico long before the Spaniards arrived and brought the dye back to Europe, where it gradually replaced kermes. Even though cochineal is the more potent dye, it still takes some 70,000 to 100,000 insects to make a pound of cochineal dye. Today, cochineal is still used to color lipsticks, pastries, and some drugs.

Cochineal's name goes back to the Greek *kokkos*, meaning "grain" or "berry," because many observers thought the tiny insects were the fruit of the plants they lived on. In 1756, the Swedish botanist Carolus Linnaeus asked a student of his to send him a sample of the cochineal bug and the plant it lived on from South America. When the plant arrived, Linnaeus was busy with his students, so the gardener took charge. He noticed that the plant seemed to be covered with some sort of pest, and cleaned the bugs off before presenting it to Linnaeus, who was quite dismayed to find not a single cochineal bug left for him to study.

Although vermilion got its name because its color so closely resembled the color produced by the "little worms" that produce kermes and cochineal, it does not come either from a worm or from an insect. Vermilion is actually made by roasting the mineral cinnabar, whose chemical name is mercury sulphide. The Chinese were probably the first to dye with cinnabar; they used it to color their oracle bones. The Italian traveler Marco Polo reported that the great Mongol ruler Kublai Khan signed his name in vermilion ink. In Sanskrit, *chinnavari* may in fact mean "Chinese red."

In the ancient world, the most important source of cinnabar was Almaden, in what is now Spain, where both Carthaginians and Romans mined cinnabar. The Romans painted statues of Jupiter with vermilion on feast days, and used the pigment to decorate bodies of heroes returning from battle in triumph. They closely regulated the mining and trade of cinnabar: under Roman law, you could not buy or sell cinnabar in Spain itself; the ore had to be sent under seal to Rome before it could be traded or roasted to extract the vermilion pigment. But people would go to great lengths to get vermilion. The Greek philosopher Theophrastus reported that in Colchis, on the Black Sea, cinnabar was found lodged in rocky crags so inaccessible that men would stand on the shore shooting arrows and hurling javelins at the cliffs to dislodge the precious ore.

Vandyke Brown *(1850)* 80
An artist's pigment made from earth dug near Cassel and Cologne in Germany and named for the seventeenth-century Flemish painter Anthony Van Dyke, who was said to have favored it.

Venetian Red *(1753)* 31
An artist's pigment named for the city of Venice and made from hematite, a stone composed primarily of iron ore, whose name comes from Greek, *lithos haematítēs*, or "blood stone." Hemoglobin, the iron-carrying pigment in blood, has the same root (see page 98).

Verdigris *(1336)* 125
An artist's pigment, from the French *vert de Grèce*, or "green of Greece." The Greeks made verdigris by exposing copper to the vapor of fermenting grape skins or by placing it in a closed cask over vinegar. Dyers used ver-

digris to make the shade they called willow green (see page 145).

Verditer *(1551)* 89
An artist's pigment made from copper carbonate, from French *vert de terre*, "green of earth."

Veronese Green *(1890)* 126
An artist's pigment, also called Terre Verte (1658), French for "green earth." The color's name comes not from the painter Paolo Veronese, but from the town of Verona, where it was dug.

Violet *(1370)* 180
The color of the flower, from Latin, *viola*, probably borrowed from the same source as the Greek name for violet, *ion*, the root of "iodine." According to one botanist, during the fifteenth and sixteenth centuries, violets were "simmered in honey, or soaked in oil, or made into a kind of marzipan with almonds and rose water, or even pickled in vinegar and sugar . . . a popular hot soup of that period was made with a broth of violet flowers, fennel seed, and savory leaves." To this day, pastry chefs decorate their creations with crystallized violets. Early chemists also used the juice of crushed violets to test whether a liquid was acid or base: acid turned the juice red; a base turned it green.

Viridian *(1882)* 130
From Latin *viridis*, "green, blooming, vigorous," ultimately from Latin *ver*, "spring."

 **is for Walnut,
Watermelon, Wintergreen,
Wisteria, and
Willow Green**

Willow Green *(1672)*   100

"Green" is an ancient color name, from the same Indo-European root as "grow" and "grass." In many cultures the words for "green" and "grow" are related: in Russian, "grass" is *trava* and an ancient word for "green" is *travyi*; in the Inuit language, "grass" is *ivik* and "green" is *iviujak*. The association makes sense, because the pigment chlorophyll, whose name means "green leaf" in Greek, both makes plants green and enables them to grow by synthesizing energy from sunlight. Chlorophyll makes plants look green because it reflects the green wavelengths of light back to our eyes; meanwhile, it absorbs the energy in the other wavelengths of light, enabling the plant to convert inorganic chemicals into organic material.

Not surprisingly, many shades of green are named for specific plants. "Willow," a tree whose branches bend and roll in the wind, comes from an Indo-European root that means "to roll" and is related to "waltz," a

145

dance with a rolling motion; and "whelk," a curving shell. Willows always grow near water, which may be the reason dowsers traditionally used willow branches as divining rods to find underground sources of water. People who live near willows, and therefore in damp places, may suffer from fevers and joint pains. To cure their "agues" (fevers) and rheumatism, people would turn to folk medicine, which often suggests that diseases and their remedies dwell side by side. By that logic, the willow, inhabitant of wet places, could well cure illnesses caused by damp. One European superstition said that you could cure rheumatism by walking three times around a willow tree as the sun was setting. Flemish peasants said the way to charm away the ague was to go early in the morning to an old willow tree, make three knots in one of its supple branches, and say, "Good morning, Old One. I give thee the cold, Old One."

Whether or not they knew it, the willow was the right place to look for help, although you needed to do more than walk around it or tie a knot in its branches. Many Native American tribes that relied on plants as their primary source of medicine used willow. Cherokees drank willow-bark tea for fever. The Creeks drank it for rheumatism, and the Inuit for sore throats. The Ojibwa, Potawatomi, Bella Coola, and Micmac peoples all used willow bark to heal sores, cuts, and bruises.

In the eighteenth century, chemists set out to discover what it was about willow bark that could cure fever and rheumatism, and to reproduce it in the laboratory. They named their discovery salicylic acid, after the willow's Latin name, *salix*, which in turn comes from the Celtic *sal lis*, "near water." Today we know a milder version of salicylic acid as aspirin, which can indeed charm away the ague.

Walnut *(1654)* 73
From Old English *wealh-hnutu*, "foreign nut"; the same root produced "Wales," the country of foreigners. (To the Anglo-Saxons, the Celtic Welsh were "foreign.") In Lithuanian legend, when the great Flood began, the god Perkun was eating walnuts, and dropped a few shells onto the rising waters. Virtuous people were able to use the shells as boats and so survived to repopulate the earth. Walnut shells are an ancient dye; the green shells turning wool yellow, the older shells coloring wool dark brown and hair black. In his *Natural History*, the Roman writer Pliny reports that the young nuts can be used to dye hair red. In seventeenth-century Germany, the wood and nuts were considered so valuable that farmers were not allowed to marry until they had planted a certain number of walnut trees.

Watermelon *(1926)* 24
The color of the fruit, a native of Africa, named for the abundance of its juice.

Wax Yellow *(1805)* 62
Old English *weax* possibly comes from a Teutonic root that means "to grow," because wax "grows" in a honeycomb; it is possibly also related to "weave," because of the honeycomb's pattern.

Wedgwood Blue *(1892)* 146
The typical color of Wedgwood pottery, which takes its name from the potter Josiah Wedgwood, Charles Darwin's grandfather.

Wheat (1711) 7

Anglo-Saxon *hwaet*, from a Germanic root that means "white" (see below), the color of ground grain.

White (950) 182

The Old English word *hwīt* comes from an Indo-European root that means "to gleam," and is related to the Russian word *svet*, "light," and the Lithuanian word *šveisti*, "to cause to shine." (See Zinc White, page 156.)

Wine (1705) 174

From Latin *vinum*, meaning both "wine" and "grape," probably related to Hebrew *yayin*, Ethiopic *wain*, and Assyrian *īnu*, all of which mean "wine" and all of which probably come from a root that means "to twine," as a grapevine does. A Persian legend tells of the origin of wine: Prince Jemshid, who loved grape juice, put several goatskin bags full of juice in the cellar of his palace. The next time he wanted a drink of juice, he opened one of the bags but the taste of the fermenting juice turned his stomach. He marked the bags as poison and forgot about them. Soon thereafter, he and his wife argued, and she decided to end her life by drinking poison. She went down to the cellar, opened one of the bags, but instead of poison she found a drink that made her giddy, and in this spirit she and her husband soon made up. When Jemshid found out what had happened, he began storing juice in his cellar on purpose, and so became the first winemaker.

Wintergreen (1926) 89

From Dutch, *wintergroen*, the plant whose leaves stay green in winter; ultimately from an Indo-European root that means "wet": winter is the wet season.

Wisteria *(1892)*

The color of the flower, named for Dr. Caspar Wistar, a Philadelphia Quaker, teacher of anatomy, midwifery, and surgery, and Thomas Jefferson's successor as head of the American Philosophical Society. Wistar held a weekly open house for scientists at his home that was attended by the eccentric British botanist Thomas Nuttall, who later named the flower to honor his host, but got the spelling wrong.

X *is for*
Xanthine Orange

Xanthine Orange *(1896)*   54

In the nineteenth century, scientists discovered that the dyeplant madder actually contained three separate pigments. They named one purpurine, after the ancient dyestuff purple (see page 118); another alizarine (see page 15); and the third xanthine, from the Greek *xanthos*, meaning "yellow" or "red-gold." The Greek poet Homer had written about a river that had two names: mortals called it Skamandros, but the gods called it Xanthos. Homer did not say why, but later writers explained that the river would dye fleeces washed in its waters red-gold or, as we might say, orange.

"Orange" comes from the Persian *nāranj*, or orange tree, and is probably related to the Tamil *naṟu*, "fragrant." Tamil, one of the oldest Indian languages, is spoken in southeast India and northern Sri Lanka, one of the earliest homes of the orange tree. In 1534 the Portuguese physician Garcia da Orta described the oranges of Sri Lanka, then called Ceylon, as "the best of the whole world in regard to sweetness and abundance of juice; one would readily give up for them all our own fruits, such as grapes and figs." In England, *nāranj* mingled with the Latin root *aureus*, meaning "gold," to give us "orange."

Oranges are native to southern China, where the fragrant fruits and blossoms were used as perfume and as incense, and to scent clothing and season vegetables. The dried peel was used in medicinal preparations; whole fruits were preserved in honey. In the year 1178, Han Yen-chih wrote a manual of citrus growing in which he said that oranges would spoil quickly if the pickers had been drinking wine that day, which is curious, because the Chinese also made an orange wine that the Chinese poet Su Tung-p'o called "worthy of turquoise ladles, silver flagons, purple gauze, and green silk wrappers."

From China people carried oranges along the great trade routes overland to India, by sea to the Malay peninsula and the east coast of Africa, and then by caravan to the Mediterranean. In medieval Italy, the town of Reggio di Calabria began a custom of holding an annual mock battle between the "uptown" and "downtown" citizens, using oranges for ammunition. Oranges flew through the air, said one seventeenth-century writer, "like giant hailstones driven by the storm." Women watched from the balconies and when the battles got too heated, they threw buckets of water on the "armies" to cool them down. (A similar battle took place in Argentina in 1932: a strike of high-school students in Tucumán got out of hand, and the local fire department was called out to hose down the rioters. The students picked oranges from the trees along the streets and pelted the firemen; when the firemen's water supply ran out, they returned fire with oranges.) European women were also known to throw oranges at men from their balconies as a token of love. In 1524, when Francis I rescued Marseilles from a siege, the women of the town showed their gratitude by showering him with thousands of oranges.

Although oranges were known in England in the thirteenth century, when the Spanish-born queen Eleanor bought seven precious oranges from a merchant ship, "orange" did not become a common color name until the sixteenth century. Until then, things we might call orange were called yellow or red or gold—even oranges. As late as 1578, the author of one herbal described the fruit's color as "golden." "Carrot red" was the name of a color in 1684, and we still call an orange shade of hair "red" today.

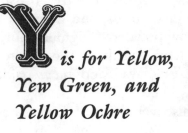 *is for Yellow,
Yew Green, and
Yellow Ochre*

Yellow Ochre *(1481)* 61

"Yellow" is one of the oldest color names in English, from an Indo-European root that means "to gleam" or "to glimmer" and also gives us the words "gold" and "yolk." "Ochre" comes from a Greek root, *ōkhros*, meaning "pale" or "wan." The poet Homer uses *ōkhros* to describe the look of fear on the face of a man in battle. "Ochre" may also be related to the Sanskrit word *vyāghrás*, or "tiger," whose color it resembles.

Yellow ochre is an ancient pigment made from the earth itself; its color comes from the presence of iron in the earth. By 35,000 B.C.E., cave painters were using yellow ochre on their walls and had already learned how to heat the pigment to change its color. When a piece of ochre was strong enough, these early artists used it like a stick of chalk, and sharpened it like a pencil. They also ground ochres on stones and mixed the powdered pigment with animal fat or bone marrow or blood to make a liquid paint. The earliest brushes were the painters' own fingers, but they also dabbed paint with sticks, perhaps chewed at the ends to create a better brush; stippled walls with pads of fur or moss; and even used hollow reeds or bones to blow powdered pigment onto wet walls. In an early form of stenciling, the painter held one hand against the cave wall and blew paint around it, leaving a clear outline of a hand.

The first cave paintings discovered in modern times are at Altamira, Spain. In 1878 a Spaniard named Marcelino Sautuola visited the Paris Exhibition, where he became intrigued by the prehistoric stone axes and arrowheads on display. He returned home and decided to investigate the caves on his own property near Santander to see if he could find any similar artifacts. These caves had been sealed by rock, but ten years earlier, the soil had shifted and exposed the entrance. One day Sautuola brought his young daughter along with him to the caves. While her father was busy examining flints on the clay floor, Maria wandered away. Unlike her tall father, five-year-old Maria was able to walk easily in the low-ceilinged cavern. Suddenly, she looked up and saw a huge wild beast staring down at her. *"Toro! Toro!"* she screamed—"Bull! Bull!" The adults came running.

Maria's bull was in fact a painting of a species of bison extinct everywhere in the world except certain forests in Lithuania. The paintings Maria Sautuola had discovered are at least 15,000 years old, and possibly older. At Altamira, and at other similar sites, painters used the natural formations of the cave walls as part of their art: curves and folds in the rock might become a bison's shoulders or the outline of a bear. A fissure in the rock might turn into the forehead of a deer. These painters also depicted human hunters, who devised the flint weapons that so fascinated Maria's father, and the animals they hunted: horses, bison, wild oxen, stags, the megaceros (a deer with giant antlers), mammoths, ibex, reindeer, the woolly rhinoceros, bears, and cave lions, as well as assorted birds, fish, and even a mysterious spotted unicorn.

Yellow *(700)* 2
See page 153.

Yew Green *(1912)* 88
Old English *īw*, probably from an Indo-European root that means "berry, grape," is related to the Latvian name for the black alder, the Old Slavonic word for willow, and an Old Icelandic word that means both "yew" and "bow." The strength and pliancy of the wood make it ideal for bows, which is why Chaucer calls it "the warlike yew."

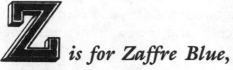 *is for Zaffre Blue,*
Zinnober Green,
and Zinc White

Zinc White *(1834)*   148

White is not, strickly speaking, a color, but the mixture
of all the colors of light in the visible spectrum. Yet we
think of white as a color, and painters need a way to de-
pict it. Over the centuries painters have used chalk,
bone, marble, oyster shells, and even eggshells to produce white pigment. In 1834 the English firm Winsor &
Newton introduced a "cool" or "bluish" white made
from zinc.

The association of zinc and white was not new. A
work attributed to Aristotle called *On Marvelous Things
Heard* mentions a mountain tribe in what is now Turkey who made a metal that "excels because of its gloss
and extraordinary whiteness." This white metal was
probably brass, an alloy of copper and zinc. The color of
brass depends on the proportion of the two metals: a
high proportion of zinc makes a very white alloy; a mixture of twenty percent zinc and eighty percent copper
produces a brass that mimics gold. This power to pro-

duce imitation gold gave zinc one of its early names, *counterfeht*, or "counterfeit."

Zinc's almost magical ability to turn copper into a metal that looked like gold fascinated alchemists who were searching for the fabled Philosopher's Stone, which would not only remove all impurities from base metals and turn them into the purest gold, but also remove all impurities, such as disease, from human beings, thereby making them immortal. When alchemists saw that zinc turned copper into a metal that looked like gold and, like gold, did not corrode, they naturally wondered whether it might be the Philosopher's Stone. Duke Julius of Braunschweig, who was obsessed by alchemy, banned the sale of zinc in his duchy, probably to prevent anyone else from creating gold or becoming immortal. (Although zinc turned out not to be the Philosopher's Stone, human bodies do require traces of zinc to sustain life.)

Paracelsus, a Swiss physician and alchemist of the sixteenth century, seems to have coined the name *Zinke*, probably after seeing zinc heated in a furnace: the metal evaporates and then forms mountainlike shapes as it condenses and cools. The German word *Zinke* is related to words that mean "spike," "jagged projection," or "pinnacle," and to the Old English word *tind*, from which we get "tine," the prong of a fork.

Europeans did not learn how to refine pure zinc until the nineteenth century, and so relied on Portuguese and Dutch traders to import zinc from Indian and Chinese metallurgists, who had understood the process of refining zinc since the sixteenth century. Not surprisingly, when Winsor & Newton developed their white pigment from zinc, they called it Chinese white. Portuguese traders called zinc *tutenago*, from the Persian word for zinc ore, *tûtiyâ*, which means "smoke," and probably refers to the way the metal evaporates during the smelting process. In England, where merchants commonly used zinc to line tea chests, a garbled version of *tutenago* became a popular nickname for zinc: "tooth and egg."

Zaffre Blue *(1662)* 138
From Italian *zaffera*, the name for cobalt blue (see page 28), possibly from Old French *safir*, "sapphire," or Arabic *ṣufr*, "yellow copper, brass."

Zinnober Green *(1895)* 130
From the German for cinnabar, the principal ingredient in vermilion (see page 141), possibly from Sanskrit *chinnavari*, "Chinese red," or Persian *shāngārf*, "red lead."

cknowledgments

I could not have written this book without the resources and helpful staff of the Massachusetts Horticultural Society Library, the Boston Public Library, the Cambridge Public Library, Simmons College Library, Wheelock College Library, the Art and Architecture Library at Yale University, and twenty-one of the Harvard College Libraries. In particular, I would like to thank Dr. Jean Cargill and the staff of the Botany Libraries; Amy Quigley, who introduced me to the joys of the computerized library search; Michael W. Gerry, president of the Boston Fine Arts Museum, who kindly let me pursue the origins of Fire Engine Red in the museum's library; Enid Allen, of Munsell Corporation; Professor JoAnn Hackett, who helped clear up a mystery about "persimmon"; and Professor Stephen Mitchell, who translated the eighteenth-century Swedish of Elisabet Christina Linnaea. Many friends were encouraging about this project, but the enthusiasm of a few stands out: Emma and Cindy, who are as passionate and curious about languages as I am; and Tom, who never tired of hearing another story about colors.

I began my searches with the most revered of all etymological dictionaries, the *Oxford English Dictionary*, 2nd edition (New York: Oxford University Press, 1989). I soon discovered that even the *OED* had its limitations: when words had Semitic roots—Arabic, Hebrew, and to a lesser extent Aramaic and Akkadian—the *OED* often said that the meaning of the root was unknown. This seemed unlikely to me, and I began to look for other etymological dictionaries. I regularly consulted Ernest David Klein's *Comprehensive Etymological Dictionary of the English Language* (New York: Elsevier Science Publishing Co., 1971), which had excellent information on Semitic roots; the *Barnhart Dictionary of Etymology* (Bronx, NY: H.W. Wilson Co., 1988); the *Oxford Dictionary of English Etymology* (Oxford: Clarendon Press, 1966); Skeat's *Etymological Dictionary of the English Language*, revised edition (Oxford: Clarendon Press, 1910); Eric Partridge's *Origins: A Short Etymological Dictionary of Modern English* (New York: Macmillan, 1966), and *Name into Word* (London: Secker and Warburg, 1949); the *Morris Dictionary of Word and Phrase Origins*, 2nd edition (New York: Harper & Row, 1988); Robert Hendrickson's *Encyclopedia of Word and Phrase Origins* (London: Macmillan, 1987); the *Bloomsbury Dictionary of Word Origins* (London: Bloomsbury, 1990); *NTC's Dictionary of Word Origins* (Chicago: National Textbook Company, 1991); Joseph T. Shipley's *Dictionary of Word Origins* (New York: Philosophical Library, 1945). When these sources disagreed with one another, I chose the explanation that made the most sense to me. In one case the etymology is my own; my sources threw up their hands about the meaning of "scotch" in "butterscotch," but the definitions of "scotch" I found provided a perfectly reasonable explanation, which I adopted.

To find names of colors, I used many sources, not least

of which were art supply stores, where I browsed the aisles, looking at the names on paints, pastels, crayons, and colored pencils. The most comprehensive dictionary of color names was compiled by Kenneth Kelly and Deane Judd in 1955: the *ISCC-NBS Method of Designating Colors and a Dictionary of Color Names*. Kelly and Judd attempted to standardize color names from many industries and sciences so that people in any field could match names to specific colors. Earlier color dictionaries did the same thing, often for a specific industry, like textiles or paints, or for a specific science, like botany or ornithology so that naturalists could agree on what they meant when they said a flower or a bird was a certain color. Of these color dictionaries, which usually came with colored plates—sometimes hand-painted—to match the color names, two discuss the origins of the names themselves at some length: Maerz and Paul's *A Dictionary of Color* (New York: McGraw Hill, 1930), which was updated in 1950; and the *Reinhold Color Atlas* (New York: Reinhold, 1961). I consulted many other color dictionaries, including Ridgway's *Color Standards and Color Nomenclature* (Washington, D.C.: n.p., 1912); the British Colour Council's *Dictionary of Colour Standards, Dictionary of Colours for Interior Decoration*, and *Wilson Colour Charts;* the Textile Color Card Association of the United States's *Standard Color Cards of America;* and the Container Corporation of America's *Color Harmony Manual.*

The most important work on color terminology in different cultures is Berlin and Kay, *Basic Color Terms, Their Universality and Evolution* (Berkeley: University of California Press, 1969), but I consulted many works that predate Berlin and Kay as well as ones that follow and often disagree with them. Among these are Grant Allen's "The Growth of the Colour-Vocabulary" in *The Colour-Sense: Its Origin and Development*, published in 1892; Au and

Laframboise's "Acquiring Color Names Via Linguistic Contrast: The Influence of Contrasting Terms" in *Child Language* #61; Nigel F. Barley's "Old English Colour Classification: Where Do Matters Stand?" in *Anglo-Saxon England* #3; "The Influence of Visual Perception on Culture" by Marc H. Bornstein in *American Anthropologist* #77; Roger W. Brown and Eric H. Lenneberg's "A Study in Language and Cognition" in *Journal of Abnormal Social Psychology*, 1954; Catherine A. Callaghan's "Miwok Color Terms" in *International Journal of American Linguistics*, vol. 45, #1; Alphonse Chapanis's "Color Names for Color Space" in *American Scientist* #53; D. A. Cruise's "A Note on the Learning of Colour Names" in *Journal of Child Language* #4; Marshall Durbin's "Basic Terms—Off Color?" in *Semiotica* #6; Umberto Eco's "How Culture Conditions the Colors We See" in *On Signs*, ed. Marshall Blonsky, 1985; E. E. Evans-Pritchard's *The Nuer*, 1940; Jane Frank's "Gender Differences in Color Naming: Direct Mail Order Advertisements" in *American Speech* 65:2; Albert Gatschet's "Adjectives of Color in Indian Languages" in *The American Naturalist* 13; Eleanor Rosch Heider's " 'Focal' Color Areas and the Development of Color Names" in *Developmental Psychology*, vol. 4, #3; Paul Kay, Brent Berlin, and William Merrifield's "Biocultural Implications of Systems of Color Naming" in *Journal of Linguistic Anthropology*, vol. 1, #1; B.J. Kouwer's "The Naming of Color Impressions" in *Colors and Their Characters: A Psychological Study* (The Hague: n.p., 1949); "Color Words in Anglo-Saxon" by L. D. Lerner in *Modern Language Review* #46; Barbara Lloyd's "Culture and Colour Coding" in *Communication and Understanding*, ed. Godfrey Vesey; E. G. Johnson's "The Development of Color Knowledge in Preschool Children" in *Child Devel-*

opment #48; Herbert J. Landar, Susan M. Ervin, and Arnold E. Horowitz's "Navaho Color Categories" in *Language*, vol. 36, #3; Eric H. Lenneberg and John M. Roberts's "The Language of Experience" in *International Journal of American Linguistics* 22; Robert E. MacLaury's "Exotic Color Categories: Relativity to What Extent," in *Journal of Linguistic Anthropology*, vol. 1, #1; N.B. McNeill's "Colour and Colour Terminology" in *Journal of Linguistics* #8; William E. Mead's "Color in Old English Poetry," *PMLA*, vol. 14, #2; Carl Mills's "English Color Terms: Language, Culture, and Psychology" in *Semiotica* 52; Verne F. Ray's "Techniques and Problems in the Study of Human Color Perception" in *Southwestern Journal of Anthropology*, vol. 8, #3, and his "Human Color Perception and Behavioral Response" in the *Transactions of the New York Academy of Sciences* 16; W.H.R. Rivers's "Observations on the Senses of the Todas," in the *Proceedings of the Psychological Society*, December 1905, and "The Colour Vision of the Natives of Upper Egypt" in *Journal of the Anthropological Institute* 31; Marshall H. Segall, Donald T. Campbell, and Melville J. Herskovits's *The Influence of Culture on Visual Perception* (Indianapolis: Bobbs-Merrill, 1966); Kenneth Shields's "Indo-European Basic Color Terms" in *Canadian Journal of Linguistics* 24:2; D. L. Snow's "Samoan Color Terminology" in *Anthropological Linguistics* 13:8; Nicole A. Steckler and William E. Cooper's "Sex Differences in the Naming of Unisex Apparel" in *Anthropological Linguistics* 22:9; H. Werner's *Comparative Psychology of Mental Development*, 1948; R. S. Woodworth's "The Puzzle of Color Vocabularies" in *Psychology Bulletin 7;* and Siegfried Wyler's *Colour and Language: Colour Terms in English* (Tübingen: Narr, 1992).

For information on pigments, dyes, and other technologies, I used Singer, Holmyard, and Hall's *History of Technology* (New York: Oxford University Press, 1954) and R. J. Forbes's *Studies in Ancient Technology* (Leiden: E. J. Brill, 1954). I also consulted works on the history of painting materials by Laurie; Mayer; and Gettens and Stout. Perhaps the most valuable single source was the journal *Ciba Review*, published in Switzerland by the Ciba chemical company. Almost every issue had something of interest, but particularly valuable were *Purple*, no. 4; *Scarlet*, no. 7; *Children's Dress*, no. 32; *Madder and Turkey Red*, no. 39; *Indigo*, no. 85; *Uniforms*, no. 93; and *Sir William Henry Perkin*, no. 115.

To track down folklore and mythology, I used Stith Thompson's *Motif Index of Folk Literature* (Bloomington: Indiana University Press, 1975); Mary Huse Eastman's *Index to Fairy Tales, Myths, and Legends* (Boston: Boston Book Company, 1915), as well as the later editions and supplements by Eastman and Norma Olin Ireland, published in 1926, 1952, 1973, 1979, and 1986; and Margaret Read MacDonald's *The Storyteller's Sourcebook* (Detroit: Neal-Schuman, 1982). I also used the *Funk and Wagnalls Standard Dictionary of Folklore, Mythology and Legend* (New York: Funk and Wagnalls, 1950); and Gertrude Jobes's *Dictionary of Mythology, Folklore, and Symbols* (New York: Scarecrow Press, 1961–62).

Readers who want to learn more about the history of English may be interested in Mario Pei's *The Story of English* (New York: Lippincott, 1952) and *The Story of Language* (New York: Lippincott, 1965); Janet Clausner's *Talk About English: How Words Travel and Change* (New York: Thomas Y. Crowell, 1990); and McCrum, Cran, and MacNeil's *The Story of English* (New York: Viking, 1986). For more on color, see Rossotti, *Colour: Why the World Isn't Grey* (Princeton:

Princeton University Press, 1983); and Augustine Hope and Margaret Walch's *The Color Compendium* (New York: Van Nostrand Reinhold, 1990).

Sources of Quotations

Amber
The Arabic legend is adapted from C. F. Akhmetov's *The Tears of the Heliades.*

Apricot
The author of the early herbal is William Turner, quoted in F. A. Roach, *Cultivated Fruits of Britain.*

The quotation about Tradescant comes from the nineteenth-century biography by Isaac Disraeli in *Curiosities of Literature.*

Aquamarine
The quotation from Pliny comes from Book 37, Chapter 20, of the *Natural History.*

Baby Blue
The quotation from *The Infant's Department* comes from "The Children's Department" by Jo B. Paoletti and Carol L. Kregloh in *Men and Women: Dressing the Part*, ed. Claudia Brush Kidwell and Valerie Steele.

The painter's manual quoted is *Bustanoby's Color Manual* by J.H. Bustanoby.

Banana
The legend of Kintu comes from Stanley's *Through the Dark Continent.*

Buff
The quotation about the coronation of James II comes from Sanford's *History of the Coronation of James II* as quoted in Cecil C.P. Lawson's *History of the Uniforms of the British Army.*

Cedar Green
The Roman writer is Pliny, in chapter 37 of the *Natural History*, as quoted in S. Tolkowsky's *Hesperides: A History of the Culture and Use of Citrus Fruits*, published in 1938.

Coffee
The legend of Kaldi is adapted from Anthony Mercantante's *The Magic Garden*.

Dapple Gray
The scientist who was told that having colors for blue and green was "highly amusing" was the Swiss ophthamologist Hugo Magnus, as quoted by Robert S. Woodworth in "The Puzzle of Color Vocabularies," published in the *Psychological Bulletin* in 1910. The response is Woodworth's.

The anthropologist who was told "There's no such beast!" is David Turton of the University of Manchester, reported in *Man*, vol. 15, #2.

Delphinium
The Pawnee legend is adapted from Vernon Quinn's *Stories and Legends of Garden Flowers*.

Emerald
The story of the goddesses is adapted from Genevieve Barlow's *Latin American Tales*.

Fire Engine Red
"I don't care what color you paint her" comes from *Enjne, Enjine: A Story of Fire Protection*, by Kenneth Holcomb Dunshee.

Flamingo Pink
The English sailor is John Sparke, quoted in volume III of *Hakluyt's Voyages*.

Flax
The legend of Hulda is adapted from Vernon Quinn's *Stories and Legends of Garden Flowers*.

Garnet

The "wonderful lustre" is from Charles de Rochefort's *History of the Carriby Islands*, translated by John Davies and published in 1666; it is quoted in Dr. Sydney Ball's article "Luminous Gems, Mythical and Real," published in *The Scientific Monthly*.

Pliny's comments on *draconitis* come from Book 37 of his *Natural History*.

The Italian physician was Camillus Leonardus; the quotation comes from *The Mirror of Stones*, which is dedicated to Caesar Borgia, quoted in Sydney Hobart Ball's *A Roman Book on Precious Stones*.

Heliotrope

"Intoxicated with delight" comes from *Flowers and Their Histories* by Alice M. Coats.

Indigo

The story of Asi comes from Esther Warner Dendel's article "Blue Goes for Down" in the Brooklyn Botanic Garden's *Natural Plant Dyeing*, Handbook II.

The quotation from the Frankfurt dyers comes from *Indigo, Ciba Review*, no. 85.

Jade

The Chinese names for jade come from *Jade Lore* by John Goette and *Adventures in Jade* by James Lewis Kraft.

Jet Black

The color terms of the Naisoi of the South Pacific are cited in Berlin and Kay, *Basic Color Terms, Their Universality and Evolution*.

The quotation from the Venerable Bede comes from Sydney Hobart Ball's *A Roman Book on Precious Stones*.

Khaki

Harry Lumsden's letter to his father is quoted in Sir

Patrick Cadell's article "The Beginnings of Khaki" in the *Journal of Army Historical Research*. Lumsden's comments about "too flash for Guides," "mud-colour," and the "most smashing regiment in India," also come from Cadell's article, as do the anecdote about the "mudlarks" and Sir Charles Napier's comments.

Lavender

The quotation about Queen Victoria comes from Donald McDonald's *Fragrant Flowers* (1895) as quoted in Reginald Peplow's *A Herbal*, published by the National Trust.

The ballad can be found in Iona and Peter Opie's *Oxford Dictionary of Nursery Rhymes*.

Lime

The quotation from Maundeville is from Tolkowsky's *Hesperides: A History of the Culture and Use of Citrus Fruits*.

Marigold

William Turner is quoted in *An English Florilegium* by Mary Grierson.

Mauve

The quotation from *Punch* comes from "Dyestuffs in the 19th Century" by E. J. Holmyard in Singer, Holmyard, and Hall's *History of Technology* (see page 164).

Nasturtium Yellow

The quotations from Elisabet Christina Linnaea come from her 1762 article *"Indianska Krassens Blickande."* Canon Russel's observations are quoted in Eric Fitch Daglish's *Marvels of Plant Life*, published in 1924.

Orpiment

The quotation from Cennini is from chapter 47 of *The Book of the Artist* in the translation of Christiana J. Herringham, published in 1899.

Oxblood
Quotation from Pliny comes from Book 33, Chapter 8, of the *Natural History.*

Pansy
Gerard is quoted in Mary Grierson's *An English Florilegium.*

Parma Violet
The quotation from Walter Savage Landor comes from Alice M. Coats's *Flowers and Their Histories.*

Persimmon
Strachey's quotation comes from his *History of Travaile into Virginia Britannia.*

Thomas Hariot wrote about the "lushious sweet" fruit in *Narrative of the First English Plantation of Virginia,* first published in 1588.

The "harsh and choakie" quotation comes from Strachey.

The sufferer who said a persimmon would "draw a man's mouth awry" is Captain John Smith, quoted in John Edwin Bakeless's *The Eyes of Discovery.*

"Raisins dipped in honey" comes from Elias Pym Fordham's *Personal Narrative,* quoted in *The Eyes of Discovery.*

Quaker Gray
The quotation about George Fox comes from Robert Hendrickson's *Encyclopedia of Word and Phrase Origins.*

William Penn is quoted in *The Quaker: A Study in Costume* by Amelia Mott Gummere, 1901.

The story about Dalton and his mother is given in several sources, including Lonsdale's *Worthies of Cumberland,* 1874, and *John Dalton and the Rise of Modern*

Chemistry by Sir Henry E. Roscoe, published in 1895. There is good reason to believe the story is apocryphal; it was told of at least one other Quaker before it was told of Dalton. Indeed, some people argued that the fairly high incidence of red-green color-blindness among Quakers was due to their lifelong habit of surrounding themselves with dull colors, but the more reasonable explanation is that Quakers tended to marry one another, and recessive traits thereby became more prevalent.

Royal Purple

The quotation from Pliny comes from Book 9, Chapter 62, of his *Natural History.*

The papyrus mentioning the stinking hands of the dyer is quoted in *The Royal Purple and the Biblical Blue*, by Isaac Herzog, edited by E. Spanier.

Ruby

The seventeenth-century writer is P. D. Rosnel, quoted in Ball's *A Roman Book on Precious Stones.*

Tobacco

The quotation about the devil comes from Benzoni, quoted by J. Alden Mason in "Use of Tobacco in Mexico and South America," the Field Museum of Natural History's Anthropology Leaflet 16.

Tomato

The quotations about Colonel Johnson come from Robert Hendrickson's *The Great American Tomato Book.*

Turquoise

The anthropologist of the Western Apache is Keith Basso, quoted in Berlin and Kay, *Basic Color Terms, Their Universality and Evolution.*

The quotation about the Zuñi cradleboard comes from Elsie Clews Parsons's *Pueblo Indian Religion*, published in 1939.

Ultramarine

The Cennini quotation is from Chapter 62 of *The Book of the Artist*, as quoted in Manlio Brusatin's *A History of Colors*.

Violet

The contemporary botanist is Peter Bernhardt in *Wily Violets and Underground Orchids*.

Willow Green

The Flemish peasants' chant comes from *Plant Lore, Legends, and Lyrics* by Richard Folkard, published in 1892.

Wine

The tale about Prince Jemshid is adapted from Ernst and Johanna Lehner's *Folklore and Odysseys of Food and Medicinal Plants*.

Xanthine Orange

The quotations from Garcia da Orta, Su Tung-p'o, and the commentator on the Battle of Reggio di Calabria (Iovanni Baptisto Ferrarii) all come from *Hesperides: A History of the Culture and Use of Citrus Fruits*.

The reference to "golden" oranges comes from Barnaby Googe's translation from the German of Heresbachius's *Four Books of Husbandry*, quoted by David Stuart in *The Kitchen Gardener: A Historical Guide to Traditional Crops*.

Yew

Chaucer is quoted in Folkard's *Plant Lore, Legends, and Lyrics*.

Zinc White

The quotation from Pseudo-Aristotle can be found in Singer, Holmyard, and Hall's *History of Technology* (see page 164).

	36		85	112	137	156	
1	37		86	113	138	157	
2	38		87	114	139	158	
3	39	61	88	115	140	159	
4	40	62	89	116	141	160	
5	41	63	90	117	142	161	
6	42	64	91	118	143	162	
7	43	65	92	119	144	163	
8	19	44	66	93	120	145	164
9	20	45	67	94	121	146	165
10	21	46	68	95	122	147	166
11	22	47	69	96	123	148	167	181
12	23	48	70	97	124	149	168	182
13	24	49	71	98	125	150	169	183
14	25	50	72	99	126	151	170	184
15	26	51	73	100	127	152	171	185
		52	74	101	128	153	172	186
17		53	75	102	129	154	173	187
18		54	76	103	130	155	174	188
	30	55	77	104	131		175	189
	31		78	105	132		176	190
	32		79	106	133		177	191
	33	58	80	107	134		178
	34	59	81	108	135		179
	35	60	82	109	136		180
			83	110			
			84	111			